# George Heiron's Travels: Midland and Western

### George Heiron's photographs
### Described by Leslie Price

The
· Transport ·
Treasury

Copyright: Images George Heiron / Transport Treasury, text: Leslie Price.
ISBN: 978-1-913251-39-0

First Published 2022 by Transport Treasury Publishing Ltd. 16 Highworth Close, High Wycombe, HP13 7PJ

www.ttpublishing.co.uk
Printed in Tarxien, Malta by Gutenberg Press Ltd

Front Cover: Morning at Bristol (Temple Meads) and in Platform 9 stands a Stanier 'Jubilee Class' 6P 4-6-0 45662 'Kempenfelt' which has just backed on to an express for Yorkshire. She has been well prepared with a 4,000 gallon tender full of water and piled high with coal; the fireman has built a substantial fire. Her safety valves are blowing ready for the 1 in 75 climb to Filton Junction, or to Fishponds with its ruling gradient of 1 in 57 at Lawrence Hill depending upon which route was being taken. Discreetly watching this from Platform 8 is George's wife Shirley; the Heirons are clearly ready for a day out by train, a regular occurrence in the 1950's. In order to construct his composition George must be standing on a porter's trolley, the handle of which is in the foreground. We shall meet 'Kempenfelt' later in the book (Images 105, 140, 141). But if the Heirons were going out for the day, what was the train on the opposite platform? If the picture was taken during the latter half of the 1950's decade, as seems likely, given the condition of 'Kempenfelt', then it would most probably be the 8.40am Bristol-Sheffield, in which case they may have been awaiting the 8.50am (8.15am ex Weston-super-Mare) to Paddington. The next question may be, 'Why was 'Kempenfelt' so named'? As we shall see later a number of the 'Jubilee' Class were named after prominent naval personnel. Rear-Admiral Richard Kempenfelt became a national hero on 12th December 1781 at the Battle of Ushant in the Bay of Biscay. He commanded a small fleet of 12 battleships which defeated a much larger French force of 19 battleships and 110 transport vessels, taking 1,620 prisoners and capturing 21 transport ships. Alas in August of the following year he was aboard HMS Royal George being repaired at Spithead when it keeled over and sank killing over 800 souls of which he was one. *GH064*

Title Page *GH0843*:

I saw the 'Devonian' running late
A handful of miles south-west of Yate
A pair of Stanier's working hard
To get their train through Stoke Gifford Yard
With Gloucester to pass and the Lickey to come
The crew were in for a testing run
Leaving ten late from Temple Meads
To make up time was their greatest needs
'Twould take all effort of pride and passion
To get to New Street in timely fashion

('Black Five' 44856 and 'Jubilee' 45573 'Newfoundland' double head 'The Devonian' past Stoke Gifford) *GH0843*

Rear Cover: From morning the day turns to evening and as the shadows lengthen at the eastern end of Temple Meads a 'Jubilee' navigates a tangle of lines on its approach to the station. She is in charge of a rake of single compartment stock coaches; those in view being of ex-LMS design. The indication from this is that it is a stopping train, probably arriving from the Midland Region, most likely Gloucester and heading for its destination, the original 1840 train shed at Temple Meads. Shadows can be deceptive and dependent upon the time of year at which the picture was taken, would indicate this is likely to be either a late autumn or early spring view. In attempting to determine which train this could be, reference to the London Midland Region Public Timetable for Winter 1960/61, the most likely contender would be the 5.40pm 'all stations' from Gloucester (Eastgate) due Temple Meads at 7.11pm. Since they were never allocated to Gloucester, this 'Jubilee' must be a Barrow Road engine on the return working of a similar outward trip from Temple Meads earlier in the day. To the right an ex-GWR 'Hall' is backing down towards the Goods Station to collect its train for an evening departure. *GH1587*

# Introduction

The first volume of George Heiron photographs published by Transport Treasury featured a selection taken on the Western Region around Bristol and further afield. But George's photography was not just limited to the Western because it wasn't just that Region that featured at Bristol. For the first half of the 1950's London Midland Region territory infiltrated into and around the city and further beyond. One of the LMR tentacles linked Birmingham not only to Bristol but Bath and Bournemouth as well. Living on the northern side of the city gave George the opportunity to take a wide range of pictures featuring some of Henry Fowler's ex – Midland Railway 'Class 2P' 'Compounds' and '4F' engines as well as William Stanier's passenger and freight locomotives.

So this second volume of his work throws the spotlight onto the London Midland Region route out of Bristol but also includes Western Region trains running on that route. All journeys with George Heiron begin, as they should at Temple Meads, so this is where our journey begins one morning. The book opens with a look at operations around Bristol followed by a visit to Weston-super-Mare to look at the holiday traffic during the 1950's. Trains of both Regions used the two northern routes out of the city via Filton and by Mangotsfield from where a trip is taken to see trains on the climb to Devonshire Tunnel at Bath. The LMR line to Birmingham was shared with the Western at various points, as far north as Cheltenham. The intriguing feature of this route was that, although it ran north it was, for the LMR the 'Up' line. This led to an interesting arrangement between Standish and Tuffley Junctions, south of Gloucester, where the 'Up' lines of each Region, as will be explained, ran in opposite directions. The journey concludes during the evening of steam at the top of the Lickey Incline.

Whilst the title of this second volume may be 'George Heiron's Travels': Midland and Western' it could just as easily have been called 'A Tribute to George Heiron' for that is what this volume is. As was illustrated in the first book, 'The Atmospheric Western', he was not just a railway photographer but also something of a social historian. Many of his photographs are unsurpassed. He used his artistry to produce pictures centring on engines, trains and railway infrastructure, in order to create images of more than just railway interest. But it wasn't just engines and trains which captured George's imagination; it was the whole of the railway environment and indeed the place of railways within the environment. He had an innate ability to create a picture of a train in the context of its surroundings.

When captioning, in order to fully appreciate his artistry, it is almost a question of putting oneself into George's shoes and look into the style he used to present them. He is telling the story of one aspect of an age as he witnessed it; to evoke, for some, now sixty plus years on, personal memories. For a younger generation it illustrates the means of travel in Britain for most of the population and goods during the middle of the twentieth century.

In a number of the photographs and given the opportunity, he would include people, whether that was railway staff, passengers (today's customers) or his wife Shirley and young son Richard, in order to bring wider interest to the picture. As austere as the 1950's were; before the advent of the 'swinging sixties', his pictures now enable us to see, post WW2, the extended lease of life for the steam locomotive with all its grace, beauty, and eventual diminishing glory. Within a handful of years from these photographs being taken, steam had been swept away.

And whilst he recorded no notes of any details of the pictures he had taken he nevertheless left a multitude of clues in them as to where a great number had been taken, so we are left to surmise and deduce where each may have been. George knew exactly where and what he was visually recording but the viewer is left trying to interpret them. In order to explain what each picture is telling us the compiler has used what evidence is available in each to take a guess at what it reveals and, using timetables, records and other books and documents of the period together with, in certain cases, Ordnance Survey Maps, a deduction where and what the exact train may be. It has to be said some are pure conjecture but it is to be hoped the viewer enjoys the mix. This book covers the period from Railway Nationalisation in 1948 through to the dawn of dieselisation.

When out on his travels, initially on his pedal cycle but on longer distances perhaps by car, there were certain places which provided the perfect opportunity for his style of photography. In consequence he would return to various Gloucestershire locations at different times to use his artistic talents to premium effect. Westerleigh, Rodway, Yate, Hall End, Wickwar and Michaelwood, are just a few of those places which afforded him a variety of different photographic opportunities. So travel with me on a second journey with George Heiron. I hope you enjoy the excursion from Bristol to Blackwell as much as I did when putting the captions together.

*Leslie Price*
Inkpen, West Berkshire, September 2022

## ACKNOWLEDGEMENTS

I would like to record my grateful thanks to Laura Birch for her work on the layout and production of this book and to Andrew Royle at Transport Treasury for his assistance in confirming a number of the locations and his other support. And last but not least to my dear wife, Patricia, for her enduring patience and encouragement.

Image 1: The best place to begin our travels with George is on the spacious forecourt of the Grade I listed Bristol Temple Meads Station, as seen from an elevated pedestrian footway at the bottom of the approach road. All the evidence he captures indicates this photograph was taken during the early 1970's. The advertisements of the Tobacconists in the foreground and on the hoardings to the right display the pricing of cigarettes in decimal currency. They were the days when cigarettes were 43 pence for a packet of twenty. The cars on view date the photograph to around 1974. Steam engines may have been eliminated by now but there is much of historical interest here. A wonderful array of period motor cars in the middle foreground recall when one could safely park on the station forecourt and go off to London by train for the day. The buses are 'Bristol RE's; a rear-engined single-decker, built by Bristol Commercial Vehicles from 1962 until 1982. They were considered one of the most successful of the first generation of rear-engined single-decker buses. The leading one is on Service No. 7 to Clifton. To the right is the W H Smith Wholesale Newspaper Distribution Centre. By 1850 the W H Smith business was recognised as the principal newspaper wholesaler in the country, a title kept to this day. Beyond is the handsome Bristol and Exeter Railway Headquarters building designed by Samuel Fripp and opened in 1854. Looking to the left we see Brunel's original Great Western Railway Terminus opened on 31st August 1840. *GH1133*

Image 2: Between 1871 and 1876, due to the number of railway companies by then using Temple Meads and the consequent increase in traffic, it was expanded into a through station. In 1878 Francis Fox constructed the cavernous canopy forming the background to this picture to complement that built at Paddington by Isambard Kingdom Brunel. Standing at Platform 9 beneath the great spanned roof is a rather dishevelled ex-LMS 'Jubilee' Class 4-6-0 45602 'British Honduras'. She is at the head of a summer 'extra' running under the Train Reporting Number (TRN) '1X48'. This type of train coding originated with a new system of TRN's introduced by The Western Region in 1960, where the letter in the code indicated the train's destination. This developed into a national four character number introduced nationally by BR in 1962, enabling us to date this photograph after that. Trains with the 'X' character referred to a 'one off' train and was generally used for various excursions or special events etc. With the first two coaches being ex- LNER designs, of which the leading one appears to be receiving some attention, the likelihood is the train is bound for Yorkshire or beyond. The engine's run-down condition suggests the picture was likely to have been taken in the latter days of steam. During the summer of 1964 'British Honduras' was based at Leeds (Holbeck) (55A) which may give a clue to the train's possible destination. Alongside in Platform 8 is a 'Class 119' Gloucester RC&W Diesel Multiple Unit set, built in 1958, forming a suburban service to Severn Beach. *GH0063*

Left Image 3: One of the hallmarks of George Heiron's work was night-time photography and this is a classic. The time exposure allows the train's pair of express headlamps to stand out, as well as those glowing along Platform 9 where a Western Region train stands, exemplified by the Churchward 'toplight' coach. The atmosphere of a quiet winter evening is captured in a single shot with this portrait of another 'Jubilee' 45605 'Cyprus' standing in Platform 12 at the head of an express. Platform 12 was one of the two platforms beneath Brunel's original train shed of 1840. As originally built it was 220 feet long but its length was almost doubled during the 1870's expansion. From nationalisation of the railways in January 1948 through to February 1964 'Cyprus' was a Leeds Holbeck (20A) based engine. She is looking in pretty good trim. This train is unlikely to be a heavy one. Throughout the steam period there was a 7.45pm (or thereabouts) (FO) express for York, originating at Bristol, which followed the 'Up' 'Midland Mail' overtaking it at Birmingham. This has the potential to be that train. By the way, it arrived at York at the unearthly time of 2.4am. The hardy passenger would only hope the Refreshment Room there was open! *GH0227*

**Opposite Bottom Image 4:** Turning the clock back we are now looking at a very early Heiron view. The 'Jubilees', post nationalisation, were the staple power for the London Midland Region (LMR) cross-country expresses. Like their forerunners, the 'Patriots', they were deemed Class 6P5F in terms of motive power and dominated this route for over a decade. This shot depicts the cleanliness and maintenance in which 'top link' locomotives were kept during the early years of the 1950's. 'Jubilee' 45570 'New Zealand' comes off its train, having just arrived in Platform 5 at Temple Meads displaying a strange headlamp code. Surely the lamp should be in the middle of the front buffer beam to signify 'a light engine'? The train is comprised of ex-LMS stock, the coach next to the tender having van end lookout windows. Additional platforms at Temple Meads, of which this was one, had been built to cope with ever increasing traffic between 1930 and 1935. Here, 'New Zealand' displays a Bristol Barrow Road (22A) shed code which she carried from Nationalisation day (01/01/1948) until May 1951 when she was transferred to Derby (17A). So we have quite a narrow window as to when this picture may have been taken. *GH1152*

**Below Image 5:** At the western end of Platform 5 we now have our first sight of 'The Cornishman', a Western Region 'named' train which arrived via Midland Region metals to get from Birmingham to Bristol. In the 1952 timetable, the name 'The Cornishman' was applied by the then Western Region to a train which left Wolverhampton (Low Level) at 9.15am and Birmingham (Snow Hill) 9.50am to Plymouth and Penzance where it was due at 5.55pm, travelling via Stratford-upon-Avon, Cheltenham (Malvern Road) and Bristol and conveying a slip portion for Taunton. By 1960 the departure time from Wolverhampton had been put back to 9.0am but an additional call was put in at Gloucester (Eastgate) and it still arrived at Temple Meads at 12.15pm as had always been the case. But during the decade the Taunton slip coach was replaced by a portion for Kingswear, detached at Exeter. 'The TRN 825' remained consistent throughout the period. The train is headed by 'Castle' 5071 'Spitfire'. This engine was delivered new from Swindon to Newton Abbot on 23rd June 1938 and after brief spells elsewhere was allocated there from July 1940 to March 1958. Originally named 'Clifford Castle' she was renamed 'Spitfire' in September 1940 in tribute to the iconic aircraft which played such a significant part in the WWII 'Battle of Britain'. The 'Cornishman' was one of those 'double home' workings, the engine and crew being Stafford Road and Newton Abbot on alternate days, the crew lodging overnight at the end of their duties at the respective destination. *GH0045*

Image 6: Not all 'LMR' summer trains were relieved by their Western counterparts at Bristol; some ran through to their ultimate destination, mostly Weston-super-Mare. Here is an example, as an ex-LMS 'Black Five' 44805 leaves Platform 3-4 with just such a train. This locomotive was out-shopped from Derby Works during June 1944 and spent the greater part of its life from Nationalisation in 1948 through to April 1965 based at Saltley, Birmingham (21A). So the train would likely to be full of holiday makers from the Midlands. This expansive view of the west end of the station is full of historical interest. The parcels dock above the locomotive's chimney owes its origin to the terminus of the Bristol and Exeter Railway whose platforms occupied this site in 1851. Adjacent to it, to the left, is that Company's Headquarters building completed in 1854. Beyond, in the background, and at right angles, is Brunel's original terminus of 1840. Then to the right is Francis Fox's canopy added in 1878. Although the locomotive is far from an example of cleanliness the coaching stock is a mixed bag mostly of ex-LMS origin which would probably indicate a picture being taken during the middle of the 1950's. *GH1154*

Image 7: Yatton is midway between Weston-super-Mare and Temple Meads. It is here George, travelling on a 'Down' train probably bound for Weston, leans out of the leading carriage window and captures this scene as his train is departing from Yatton. On the right is the handsome 129 lever Yatton West Signal Box, with its intricate filigree bargeboards, and approaching it in the 'Up' direction a 'Stanier Black Five' 45333 at the head of a summer extra train. It is carrying an improvised Western Region 'TRN 244'. The point of conjecture here is; where did this LMR engine pick up the train? In the latter half of the 1950's 'TRN 244' was the designated summer number for the 08.25am Ilfracombe to Manchester (Exchange). The train would have come across the Western branch line from Barnstaple and the locomotive change would then have taken place at Taunton. The train may also be carrying a portion from Minehead. The locomotive looks well kempt for passenger work and appears to carry an 'A' shed code plate, which again cannot be faithfully identified. A fascinating feature of the picture is the signalman's footboard crossing in the foreground; which enabled him to safely cross the main lines to give a Cheddar line driver, diverging to the left, the single line token. *GH0739*

Image 8: Weston-super-Mare was blessed with two stations during the period of these photographs. On the right of the picture a train moves into Locking Road, the excursion station used during peak periods for originating and terminating trains. In this picture, beyond the coaches, we have sight of the turntable and watering facilities provided at Locking Road. Meanwhile an unidentified 'Hall' slowly moves its heavy express out of the General station. It is displaying two 'TRN's','H1' on a bracket obscuring the engine's smoke box number plate and another, 'TRN 1M14', chalked at the top of the smoke box door. It is an illustration of the development of Train Reporting Numbers. This would have kept the signalman in Weston-super-Mare East Box guessing and all other Boxes along the route! How were they going to reconcile the TRN's with their Working Timetables (WTT) or Weekly Notices? The TRN on the bracket using a letter was introduced by the Western Region for the 1960 Summer Timetable which was followed from July 1962 by the introduction nationally of the four digits TRN, as shown by the chalked number (See also Image 11 for further information). So it may be deduced this photograph was taken in summer 1962. The best indication of the train's destination is the letters M and H. The 'M' indicates a destination in the Midland Region and more specifically the 'H' indicates the Birmingham or Worcester Districts. In the previous year's TRN list 'M14' related to the 9.10am (SuO) Penzance-Wolverhampton. If we put that circumstantial evidence together '1M14'could be this train. *GH0738*

Image 9: We have now arrived at Weston-super-Mare General and judged by the number of passengers making their way to the station exit, the train standing in Platform 1 may have just arrived? An indication is that nobody is rushing to board; it was the custom of the day to await an announcement before boarding a train, just in case one may end up at an unexpected destination. A similar picture to this appeared in Volume 1 –'The Atmospheric Western' which could have been taken at much the same time; quite likely a summer Saturday. From that picture we know that the time was about 11.0am. The train would have to go to the Locking Road Carriage Sidings for cleaning or else be cleaned whilst standing at the platform before making its return working. From the coach number which can be partially seen, 'W260XX' we may assume this is an internal Western Region service. The grouping in the left foreground is perhaps a typical early 1960's family, Mum with her rafia basket, Dad and four children. There is also Grandad, in his cloth cap and is this Grandma seated in the right foreground? The platform notice in the immediate foreground is 'Ladies Waiting Room'; would this be politically correct in the present day of Unisex Waiting Rooms (& Toilets)? The little girl's knee length white boots known as 'go-go' boots became a fashion item in the early 1960's. This strikes me as a London family and fascinatingly, in the 1960 timetable 'TRN A51' was the 11.05am (SO) Weston-Paddington which may have persisted in following years. GH0743

Image 10: If it were not for all the steam being jettisoned from one of the locomotives this would be a comprehensive view of Weston's two stations; but it is the steam which makes the picture different. On the left the engine making all that steam is 'Castle Class' 7022 'Hereford Castle' making a very determined departure from the main station. She is displaying an express train headlamp code so she is 'right-away Temple Meads'. Meanwhile an unidentified ex- LMS 'Jubilee', which had probably arrived at Locking Road from the north earlier, has now been relieved of its train and has backed down to the station neck in order to access the turntable and servicing facility by means of the line disappearing out of the picture to the right. Note the water tank lid on the tender has already been opened. Controlling these events is Weston-super-Mare East signal box partially shrouded by the steam. Unusually for an ex-GWR signal box, until 1955 it was called Weston-super-Mare No.1 but was renamed on the closure of the much smaller Weston-super-Mare West box. The loop line via Weston-super-Mare was singled on 31st January 1972 which spelt the end for this former 113 lever box. Its original 1955 cast iron GWR name board sold at auction for £1,000 in July 2021. The '70xx Class' were the last of the 'Castles' to be introduced from 1946; but 'Hereford Castle' was not delivered from Swindon until 15th June 1949, by then post-nationalisation. She is carrying a Plymouth Laira (83D) shed code plate which suggests the train is probably a West of England – Bristol working. *GH0742*

Image 11: This picture shows the spaciousness of the excursion platforms at Locking Road. At one of those stands a train headed by 'Jubilee' 45725 'Repulse' displaying 'TRN 1E68' on its smoke box door. In 1960 a transition began to take place regarding Train Reporting Numbers when the Western Region introduced destination letters. During that and the following summer 'TRN E68' applied to the 12.04pm Weston-super-Mare – Sheffield (Midland); the 'E' indicating a destination in the Eastern Region. From July 1962 BR changed the Headlamp Codes displayed by locomotives from an alphabetic system to a numeric one in order to formulate a national four character 'TRN'. What was formerly a Class 'A' (express train) became a Class '1'. Therefore it is fairly safe to deduce that 'E68' became '1E68' for the 1962 summer season. This train was also designated as a 'Q' train (Only runs as required), which in this case was on summer Saturdays at the height of the holiday season. 'Repulse' had been based at Sheffield (Millhouses) (19B) throughout the 1950's but on the closure of that shed on 31st December 1961 she was put into storage. She was returned to traffic at Sheffield (Darnall) between 23rd June and 29th December 1962 for the summer season and the last six months of her service. She was scrapped at Cashmore's, Great Bridge, Birmingham in March 1964. *GH0754*

Image 12: Locking Road, an addition to the General, was opened by the Great Western Railway in 1914, just before the outbreak of the First World War, to deal with the then burgeoning excursion traffic. It reached its peak during the 1950's when, on summer Saturdays all four platforms came into use with throngs of holiday makers crowding the station. The number of diesels in the background suggests this picture was taken during the early 1960's, by which time such traffic was rapidly declining. The uncared for 'Jubilee' 45564 'New South Wales' was a long term resident at Leeds (Holbeck) (20A) from August 1953 through to July 1964 so there is little doubt where this train is heading. The summer edition of the LMR timetable for 1963 shows trains leaving at various times for Newcastle, Sheffield and Bradford so this could be any one of them. It is difficult to understand in this day and age how far people would travel in the 1950'/60's just to experience a day or short weekend at the seaside. With the decline of holiday traffic by rail, the excursion platforms at Locking Road closed at the end of the summer season on 6th September, 1964. *GH0741*

Image 13: In this view taken from the same road over bridge we have a much clearer view of the 113 lever Weston-super-Mare East signal box. The sun shines; the air is clear but, as in the previous picture (12), the safety valves are blowing. This time it is on a 'Hall Class' 4996 'Eden Hall' as it pulls away from the General Station with TRN 'T33'. What does this tell us? In the 1960 summer timetable the letter 'T' indicated a train terminating in the Western Region Districts of Newport or Gloucester. Records do not show where the train originated; it may even have been here at Weston but the fact it is leaving from the main station rather than Locking Road suggests it may have been from further afield. However given the 'T' destination letter it is likely bound for Newport, Gloucester or more likely Cheltenham. The fact the 'TRN' has been chalked or painted directly onto the smoke box door indicates it is not a regular summer extra but a train arranged at short notice. 'Eden Hall' was allocated to Worcester (85A) between November 1959 and July 1961 which may give a clue as to its destination. In the background note the severe curvature of the 'Up' platform. Because of this the driver could never see the Guard's green flag. So on the guard's whistle, 3 or 4 porters would position themselves along the train. Starting from the front, they would check the doors and, if OK, raise their arm facing back down the train. When the sequence of raised arms reached the guard he would wave the green flag. The porters, still with raised hands, would in turn reverse their positions to give the 'right away' to the engine driver. *GH0749*

Image 14: Back at Bristol we have an early morning view at Temple Meads; the Heirons were clearly having a day out. George's wife, Shirley is adorned in an outfit of the day and graces the picture at the eastern end of Platform 8. The three engines in view are all pure Great Western. On the right side of the picture a Hawksworth 'County Class 1000 'County of Middlesex' pulls away from Platform 9 with an 'Up' express. On one of the through lines stands a George Churchward '2800 Class' (Heavy Freight) 2881, waiting for a clear road, and lurking in the gloom of the train shed in Platform 8, hiding behind the water column, is another Churchward designed locomotive '4300 Class' 6391. As well as carrying an 'Express' headlamp code 'County of Middlesex' displays a Bath Road (82A) shed plate. She was allocated here between late February 1954 and September 1960. By the time of her withdrawal from service on 6th July 1964 she had covered almost three-quarters of a million miles. '2881' was allocated to Newton Abbot from May 1950 until January 1960 when it was withdrawn. As for '6391', lurking in the background, it was based at one or other of Bath Road (82A) or St.Philip's Marsh (82B) between April 1955 and early 1959. When it was withdrawn in September 1962 it had recorded over one and a quarter million miles and by the time of their demise both of the latter engines had been in service for over forty years. From these dates we are able to conclude the picture would have been taken during the second half of the decade. *GH0057*

Image 15: This is another example of a classic Heiron night-time photograph. Standing at Platform 8 at Temple Meads is a resplendent '6959 Class Modified Hall' 7919 'North Aston Hall'. This Class, a development of Charles Collett's original 'Hall Class' from 1924, was designed by Frederick Hawksworth and introduced from 1944. But 'North Aston Hall' was not released from Swindon Works until 21st April 1950, more than two years after the railways were nationalised. Whether this photograph was taken soon after its release or a subsequent overhaul is a matter of conjecture. She is carrying a 'stopping train' headlamp code so could be on a regular 'running-in' turn. The stopping service between Swindon and Bristol was regularly used for such turns so here '7919' could be heading a return to Swindon. The last such stopping train of the day left Temple Meads at 5.45pm running via Badminton and calling at all stations. In the adjacent refuge siding is a Travelling Post Office (TPO) vehicle with its mail collection bag on show. This 50ft. long vehicle was built by the Great Western Railway in the early 1930's and was still in use late into the 1950's decade. The 'Midland TPO' left Bristol at varying times between 7.20pm and 7.25pm throughout the decade and the TPO's would be stabled here in advance of the arrival of the 'Up North Mail' from Penzance around 7pm. *GH0059*

Image 16: The departing 'Up' Cornishman comes under scrutiny from a pair of young train spotters standing on the slope of Platform 8 as it makes a strident effort to get its heavy train on the move. The **TRN** 'H32' headcode for 'The Cornishman' was introduced by the Western Region for the summer timetable in 1960, which showed a departure time from Temple Meads as 4.8pm. As previously explained this headcode persisted until the introduction of the four digits headcode in June 1962. The locomotive, displaying a Stafford Road (84A) shed plate, looks remarkably like 'Castle' 7019 'Fowey Castle'. According to **SLS** records she was allocated at '84A' from May 1961 until September 1963. On the closure of Stafford Road on 9th September 1963 she was re-allocated to the other Wolverhampton shed, Oxley (by then 2B). She was noted entering Swindon Works on 17th March 1964 to undergo an 'Unclassified Overhaul' from which she emerged just less than two months later on 8th May 1964. Alas, less than nine months later, she was withdrawn and condemned at Oxley on 13th February 1965, one of the last few 'Castles' left in active service. 'Fowey Castle' is about to pass another 'Castle' 4075 'Cardiff Castle', sitting in the refuge siding awaiting its turn to pick up another express coming in from the West. This would probably have been a Paddington train because this engine was based at **O**ld **O**ak **C**ommon (81A) from 4th November 1959 until 3rd November 1961 when she was withdrawn, pinpointing this as a photograph taken during the summer of 1961. *GH0055*

Image 17: At the eastern end of the station clouds hang heavy over Temple Meads. In this wonderful view, taken from the roof of Hare's Rainbow Paint Factory we see a 'BR Standard Class 5' 73038 making a stirring exit from Platform 9 with what appears to be a summer extra or excursion train. Its stock is a mixture of ex-LMS coaches of various periods. The engine's appearance looks as though it could do with some attention considering that it was only released into service from Derby Works in September 1953. It was noted as being back there in the early months of 1959, undergoing overhaul and back in the Erecting Shop yet again during September 1961. It is carrying a hastily prepared type of the same 'TRN' introduced in 1960 which would suggest the picture was taken around that time. George has constructed the composition around its backdrop, showing off the layout of the station to good effect. On the extreme left an ex-GWR Pannier tank sits beside the Loading Bank. Behind this engine are the platforms of the 1930's extension to the station. Then to the right is the canopy of 1878 followed by Brunel's original train shed from 1840. On the right is the massive Great Western Goods Depot in front of which is the diminutive Goods Yard Signal Box, seen above the second and third coaches of the train. *GH1615*

Image 18: George was up very early for this photograph; notice the brightness in the sky and the shadow cast over the bay extension of the 1930's designed Art Deco Bristol East Signal Box. Both notify the sun is in the east even if some of the clouds do not bode well. As with the previous image 17 this was taken from the flat roofed extension to Hares Rainbow Paints Factory just outside the eastern end of the station and the perfect vantage point. The train headed by an unidentified 'Jubilee' appears to have the points set for the Midland route out of Bristol although the signal indication cannot be properly distinguished. The first four vehicles of the train are pure Gresley LNER stock dating back to the 1930's and even earlier to Great Northern Railway design. In 1941 Edward Thompson followed Nigel Gresley as the CME of the LNER and continued to develop the designs of Gresley in coaching stock. The detailed differences were that Gresley's vestibule carriages had domed roof ends and square ended toilet windows as distinct to Thompson's straight roof ends and oval windows. These then are definitely Gresley's. Both persisted in use into the 1960's due to their versatility in being able to link with more modern stock i.e. BR Mark 1 coaches. *GH1590*

Image 19: Another picture, taken from almost in front of Bristol East Signal Box during an evening sunset sees a 'Jubilee' 45659 'Drake' pulling out of Temple Meads at the head of an express. The time of day and with two BR Mark 1 Brake Vans, heading the consist of the train, can really only lead to the conclusion this is the 7.25/7.30pm (depending on the year this photograph was taken) Bristol- Newcastle mail train setting out on its nine hour journey to Newcastle. The condition of the engine suggests this would likely be an early 1960's view. 'Drake' was based at Leeds (Holbeck) (20A) from at least nationalisation (01/01/1948) to May 1963. Being Leeds based suggests 'Drake' would be working the train through to that point before an engine change took place. She remained working main line duties from Holbeck right up to her demise, being noted at Glasgow (Corkerhill) (67A) in steam on 14th April 1963. Corkerhill was the shed used by engines arriving at Glasgow (St Enoch) via the Settle and Carlisle line and the Glasgow & South-Western route via Dumfries and Kilmarnock. The presence of the engine there implies it probably would have worked a St. Pancras – St. Enoch express forward from Leeds; quite likely the overnight sleeper or the 'Thames-Clyde Express'. Just over a month after that sighting she was withdrawn from Holbeck on 24th May 1963. *GH1170*

Image 20: We now catch our first sight of the 'The Devonian'. Although this was an **LMR** named express it was inter-regional, originating at Paignton and travelling through to Bradford (Forster Square). Ironically it used the Western Region route out of Bristol as far as Yate. Here the double headed train rounds the curve into Dr. Day's Bridge Junction, the pilot engine being a 'Black Five' 44848. This was a Derby (17A) based locomotive from October 1955 to January 1959 so it could be safe to assume this picture was taken sometime during this period. As was usual for the time the train engine is a 'Jubilee'; but as the engine cannot be identified, it nevertheless does give us an impression of what the 'Devonian' would have looked like during the second half of the 1950's decade. During the early part of the period the traditional departure was from Kingswear at 9.00am. But by the summer season of 1963 the weekday train had been pared back to Paignton with a departure time of 9.30am. Only on Saturdays did it start from Kingswear leaving at 9.10am then running 'fast' from Torquay all the way through to Burton-on-Trent, due there at 3.30pm. As on weekdays, an engine change between Western Region and Midland power had to be effected at Bristol. The misnomer, 'ran fast' is exemplified in the timetable on a Saturday, which shows the weekday train arriving at Derby at 3.21pm whereas on Saturdays it arrived at 3.49pm! The Saturday train was also strengthened, requiring double heading from Bristol. The change of motive power from Western to Midland must have taken place somewhere beyond the station limits. Note the enthusiastic train spotters hanging over the wall on the left. *GH0759*

Image 21: Taken from the same road bridge but the opposite side of the tracks; a panoramic view of Dr. Day's Bridge Junction, with the southern suburbs of Arnos Vale and Brislington on the hillside in the background. Around the Bristol Loop from Feeder Bridge Junction comes a Hawksworth 'County Class' 1001 'County of Bucks' with what is very likely to be a South Coast to Cardiff express. In a timetable of the period there were three such trains. The long shadows and evening atmosphere suggests this could be the 5.35pm Salisbury to Cardiff, which picked up a connection at Salisbury from Southern Region trains starting all the way back at Hastings (depart 12.45pm). This locomotive would have worked the train through from Salisbury, calling at Stapleton Road at 7.34pm. Routing trains this way avoided having to reverse direction at Temple Meads, saving time and operational difficulties. Connections to Temple Meads were available at Stapleton Road. At that station the 'running-in board' actually read "Bristol Stapleton Road change for South Wales, Clifton and Avonmouth". 'County of Bucks' was allocated to Neyland (87H) in West Wales from October 1948 right through to January 1961. Whether this train was part of a Neyland shed roster or the engine was being used by Cardiff (Canton), as a filling in turn, is a matter of conjecture. It was withdrawn on 24th May 1963 after a short service life of only seventeen years, eight months and twelve days during which time it had covered 664,361 miles. *GH0762*

Image 22: The Western Route took 'The Devonian' up the 1 in 75 gradient from Dr. Days Bridge Junction to Filton Junction, an all-out effort for northbound trains climbing out of Bristol. In this shot we see another double-headed train assaulting the bank at Narroways Cutting on the 'Up' fast line. The carriage headboard (Bradford-Paignton) suggests this is 'The Devonian'. Running beside it on the 'Up' slow is another passenger train comprising ex-LMS coaches which could be a West and North express taking the Bristol and South Wales Union line at Filton Junction; heading for the Severn Tunnel. The train engine of 'The Devonian' is a clean looking 'Jubilee' 45563 'Jervis' piloted by a less well presented 'Black Five'. 'Jervis' was based at Bristol Barrow Road (22A) from nationalisation through to January 1958 when it went to Derby (17A) until October 1959. The coach carrying the headboard is a BR Mark 1. These types of coaches were first introduced by BR in 1951 to gradually replace the ageing stock of the 'Big Four' railway companies. Right through the 1950's some locomotives were kept in tip-top condition for working the crack expresses. But what is a Midland Region train doing on the Western Region route north out of Bristol which would have increased its journey time by seven minutes over the Midland route? A possible explanation involving the other named express, 'The Cornishman' will follow later. (See Image 41) *GH0909*

Image 23: The bridge that 'the Devonian' was just about to pass beneath, featured in the previous Image 22, carried the old Clifton Extension Railway between Kingswood Junction and Ashley Hill Junction, jointly owned by the Great Western and Midland Railways. This route formerly connected the ex-Midland Railway to the GWR Avonmouth and Severn Beach branch, giving the Midland access to Avonmouth Docks. George captured this evening photograph at Narroways Cutting featuring one of Henry Fowler's ubiquitous ex-LMS 4F 0-6-0 locomotives, introduced from 1924; a development of his original design from 1911. Fowler was the Chief Mechanical Engineer of the Midland Railway and subsequently LMS, from 1909 until his retirement in 1933. During this time 738 of his design of goods engine were built. Number 44424 was built at Derby in 1927 and shedded at Barrow Road (22A) from Nationalisation through to October 1959. It was eventually withdrawn from service at Stoke (5D) in October 1963. The Class's longevity speaks volumes for their utility and versatility. Here '44424' was very likely being employed on a goods train of sheeted wagons from Westerleigh Yard to Avonmouth Docks. *GH1080*

Image 24: From an elevated position at the northern end of Narroways Cutting, George recorded this view of the northbound 'Devonian'. From the evidence of the shadows we may deduce it was taken on a fine winter or early spring day. Note to the top left of the photograph the extent to which allotments were popular during this period; they do not yet appear to have been set for the forthcoming year. This picture illustrates a strengthened 'Devonian' climbing Filton bank, heading towards Ashley Hill Station. The train engine, once again, is piloted by a 'BR Standard Class 5.' The usual consist of the weekday 'Devonian' was eight/nine coaches but on Saturdays and at peak periods this would often be extended to ten or more. In order to navigate Filton Bank and the Lickey Incline, an additional train engine would be required from Bristol, as illustrated here. Although the platforms at Ashley Hill extended over all four tracks it was but a Bristol suburban station and during this period was not particularly busy. It closed on 23rd November 1964. However in January 2018, it was revealed that there were plans for reopening the station (although now referred to as Ashley Down) as part of 'Metro-West', the reopening of the Henbury Spur, one of Bristol's transport regeneration schemes. *GH0911*

Image 25: A wonderfully nostalgic scene full of atmosphere, from the austere days of the 1950's; it looks somewhat bleak and cold, except for the boiler of 'Jubilee' 'Jervis' again, glistening in the low sun, attacking Filton Bank. This then is decidedly a mid-winter shot, when the sun only rises marginally above the yardarm. We are now somewhere in the vicinity of the platform ends of Ashley Hill Station looking south towards Temple Meads; note the 'PASSENGERS are not allowed to CROSS the RAILWAY except by the BRIDGE' notice in the bottom left hand corner. In the cold and low light the engine's express headlamps glow and in the foreground, the runner beans have withered on their rickety sticks in the allotment. The other sign to the left reads 'CYCLING ON THIS PATH STRICTLY PROHIBITED'. Clearly the very well wrapped up man on his bicycle is blithely ignoring it (surely there must have been a similar sign at the other end of the path!). And is the partly seen cycle, parked against the fence beside the sign, George's trusty steed? Close inspection of the photograph reveals that 'Jervis' is carrying a headboard at the top of its smoke box door and the only train that this could contend for is 'The Devonian'. This train plied its trade all year round between Yorkshire and Devon for forty eight years from 1927 to 1975. Throughout the 1950's the northbound train left Paignton daily around 9.30am; in winter as in this picture, loaded to eight coaches, it left Temple Meads around 12.45pm. *GH0910*

Image 26: At Filton junction 'The Devonian' rounded the east fork towards London where, shortly after joining the South Wales - Paddington main line, it ran through the Western Region Marshalling Yard at Stoke Gifford. It is here we now get a panoramic view of the train hastening through the somewhat deserted sidings. On this occasion the train is loaded to ten coaches and double headed by a 'Black Five' 44856 piloting a 'Jubilee' 45573 'Newfoundland', both types designed by Sir William Stanier. Equally both engines were regulars on this route and together based at Leeds (Holbeck) (20A) between January 1948 and August 1953. '44856' then moved on to spells at Derby (17A) and Saltley (21A) whereas 'Newfoundland' remained at Leeds right through to September 1965 when she was withdrawn. Overlooking the site on the north side stands the tower of St. Michael's Church, Stoke Gifford. The Yard was constructed and opened in 1903 as part of the newly built Great Western South Wales Main Line, more familiarly known as the 'Badminton Route'. In 1918 it was enlarged to ten longer sidings on each side providing a total capacity for 1,473 wagons. Three cripple sidings capable of holding a further 87 wagons were added on the 'Up' side. The vastness of the Yard is shown to full effect here but by this period wagon load traffic was going into decline and it now looks half empty. In October 1971 the Yard closed for the purpose of marshalling traffic and Bristol Parkway station was built on much of the 'Up' side, opening on 1st May 1972. Some of the sidings on the 'Down' side were subsequently used for wagon storage. *GH0842*

Image 27: This **BR Standard Class 9 2-10-0 92135** is standing in what appears to be the '**Up**' loop at **Stoke Gifford Yard**. It seems to be the subject of some debate amongst the shuffle of shunters gathered around it. The safety valves are blowing wildly which indicates the fireman has prepared the engine well for its impending departure. It displays a '**Class 5**' headlamp code; one top and one left on the buffer beam as viewed from the front. This then is an '**Express freight train with the automatic (vacuum) brake operative on not fewer than half of the vehicles**'. In railway parlance this means a through freight of mixed vehicles, with some vans and wagons vacuum fitted and the remainder not. '**92135**' was delivered new from **Crewe Works** on 30th June 1957 and went direct to **Saltley (21A)** where it was based until May 1966. With this engine on the front this freight would probably be quite a heavy train which, with Saltley shed being near **Washwood Heath Yard** in Birmingham, may indicate where the train was bound. In March 1961 '**92135**' was noted outside the **Erecting Shop** at Crewe Works either awaiting an overhaul or else coming out after one. Was this a consequence of the above discussion or was it for a scheduled overhaul? We shall never know. Whatever, it had a life of only ten years being withdrawn in June 1967 and scrapped nine months later at **Draper's Yard, Hull.** *GH1553*

Image 28: Viewed from the signal box steps at Westerleigh Junction, 'The Devonian' is taking the northbound Westerleigh curve. By the early 1960's', as a named express, it was beginning to lose its prestige. Although there is no visible escape of steam from tell-tale places, outwardly 'Jubilee' 45699 'Galatea' has a somewhat dishevelled appearance. She was based at Barrow Road (22A) from May 1948 until 1961, by which time diesel power was increasingly displacing steam. It is reported in Stephenson Locomotive Society records that on 31st August 1961 she was one of six Barrow Road 'Jubilees' reallocated to Shrewsbury (89A). In return Barrow Road received a single locomotive from Shrewsbury, BR Standard Class 5 73094, whilst three others of the same Class, '73091/92/93' were sent to Gloucester (Barnwood) in return. It was a practical sign of the times. This date probably signifies when steam traction ceased on 'The Devonian'. It is probably safe to assume this photograph dates to that period. However that was not the end of the line for 'Galatea'. She continued in service at Shrewsbury until November 1964 when she was withdrawn. Then going into store at Eastleigh Works in December 1964, she remained there until January of the following year when it seemed her time was up. But she was then moved by rail to Woodham's scrap yard in Barry; and subsequently rescued by preservationists. As of 2019 she was again operating on the main line, working railtours in the northwest of England as part of the West Coast Railway fleet. *GH1331*

Image 29: From exactly the same steps George recorded an ex-GWR 'Hall', 6995 'Benthall Hall' running on to the Westerleigh Curve with a special train. As the **TRN** indicates this was 'Z10'. It has not been possible to determine which specific train this headcode referred to. As previously stated this type of headcode had initially been introduced by the Western Region in 1960 and in 1962 was further developed to become the basis of national Train Reporting Numbers which is still in use today. In this case the letter 'Z' in the code denoted this train was a special or excursion for a destination somewhere within the Western Region. Being a late addition to the timetable the train would not have appeared in the standard Working Timetable but in the Weekly Notices, the contents of which was the responsibility of every signalman to make himself fully aware. In May 1964 'Benthall Hall' was transferred from Cardiff East Dock (88L) to Gloucester (Horton Road) (85B) and was based there for only six months until, in September 1964, she was re-allocated to Worcester (85A). Note the difference in appearance between this engine and the 'Jubilee' in the previous Image 28. Despite her condition in this photograph she was condemned at Worcester just six months later, in March 1965, at a time when all remaining ex-GWR Locomotives were systematically being withdrawn. With that in mind we may assume this photograph would have been taken between May 1964 and March 1965 and the train was probably destined to one or other location. *GH1333*

Image 30: It takes a determined photographer to get a shot like this and George most certainly fell into that category. As has previously been stated, he was 'A man for all seasons'. He seemed to have taken on all the challenges photography can present. For this photograph he would have cycled two or three miles from his home along snow covered lanes to obtain a result such as this. It is an outstanding photograph. It also shows it took a lot to stop the railways running back in the 50's and 60's. In the depths of winter, with skies full of dark snow laden clouds, an ex-LMS Stanier 8F 48460 comes off the Westerleigh curve to join the westbound Western Region main line at Westerleigh Junction. Displaying a 'Class 6' headlamp code - one middle and one to the right of the buffer beam, as viewed from the front - signifies 'an express freight partly fitted with the automatic (vacuum) brake operative on not fewer than 20 per cent of the vehicles'. The vans immediately behind the engine's tender would have been so fitted. '48460' was based at Stourbridge Junction (84F) from March 1961 until July 1966, so this scene could have been taken during the very harsh winter of 1962/63 when snow lay on the ground all the way through from Boxing Day until the following March. This freight from the Midlands was probably bound for Stoke Gifford Yard. *GH0727*

Image 31: On another cold but clear winter day an unidentified Stanier 'Black Five' rounds the north to west curve at Westerleigh and, having just 'got the road', opens up at the Junction with the Western Region main line. The headlamp code on the engine's front buffer beam indicates it is in charge of a 'Class 4' Express freight train 'pipe fitted throughout with the automatic vacuum brake operative on not less than ninety per cent of the vehicles', or as was commonly called, 'a fully fitted freight'. It is quite a heavy train which mainly appears to consist of four wheeled vans which could be another trainload from the West Midlands to Stoke Gifford Yard. The Westerleigh Junction 'Down' home signal, that it is about to pass, is pure Great Western with its lower quadrant arm and finial embellishment on top of the post. Another signal can be seen in the distance behind the train's brake van next to the 'Up' line. This is the Junction's 'Up' advanced starter. Such a signal was used at a location where it might be desirable to advance a train from a station platform or junction before the next section became available. This permitted the Westerleigh signalman to allow a train to draw forward beyond the junction toward the advanced starting signal, which controls entry to the section ahead, enabling the junction itself to be cleared for trains on the main line behind it to pass undelayed. *GH1265*

Image 32: Viewed from the 'Up' track a little further north another very heavy 'Down' train rounds the Westerleigh curve past the advanced starter signal referred to in the previous image 31. This double-header, displaying a Train Reporting Number, '3X06', also carries a 'Class C' headlamp code indicating this is a train of perishables, requiring some priority. From what can be seen it is loaded to at least sixteen bogie vehicles; there could be more. There is only one kind of train this could possibly be in the middle of summer and that is a 'Pigeon Special'. It is probably difficult now to imagine how popular 'Pigeon Racing' was during the 1950/ early 60's period. It provided a good source of revenue for the railways until this traffic succumbed to road transport in the middle of the 1960's. The Somerset and Dorset was a popular destination for such trains but this one is on the Westerleigh loop, rather than the Midland main line via Mangotsfield to Bath, so could be destined to a release point on the Western Region somewhere beyond Bristol. Both locomotives are 'Black Fives' and the pilot engine '45270' displays a Crewe South (5B) shed code plate; perhaps this was where the train was marshalled. It was allocated there from nationalisation until late December 1960 except for a three months spell at Llandudno Junction (6G) during the preceding summer. Note the seventh vehicle behind the tender, a BSK, probably provided for race officials to accompany the pigeons and supervise their release. *GH1315*

Image 33: Another photographic technique George was eager to perfect was 'panning', which gives the train an appearance of speed passing through the landscape. Among other places, he used Westerleigh curve in his earliest attempts to hone his craft. Here he has chosen a 'Black Five' 44856 piloting a 'Jubilee', the number of which cannot be discerned. When panning a photograph the photographer has to focus on one particular feature, in this case the cab side number of the 'Black Five' 'engine. In consequence the features of the 'Jubilee' are blurred but we can see it is carrying a headboard and this once again can only be 'The Devonian'. '44856' spent most of its life on the Bristol to Birmingham main line. From August 1953 to November 1959 it was based at Derby (17A) and then at Saltley (21A). Apart from a few months at Nottingham it remained at Saltley until May 1963. We last saw this engine at Stoke Gifford in Image 26. Given how well turned out the train engine is, it is probable it was one of the Barrow Road based 'Jubilees'. Taking these facts into consideration this would indicate a late 1950's photograph. Whenever piloting was required for 'The Devonian' it was usually a Saltley engine that provided it. *GH0018*

Image 34: A little further around the curve this photograph portrays a 'block oil train', a familiar sight on the railways during the early years of the 1960's. Whilst at the time it was providing very valuable income for BR, at the same time, it was contributing to the railway's demise. From the locomotive's wheel arrangement we can see the train is headed by a Stanier Class 8F 2-8-0. Note also the regulatory two open wagons acting as a barrier between the oil tanks and the steam locomotive. The multi-national oil company Exxon Mobil had an oil terminal at Avonmouth with one hundred and ninety storage tanks. They also had a distribution centre in Birmingham with seventeen tanks in constant need of replenishment. This would be the type of train which carried out the function of delivering the oil from one to the other. The tanks are marked as carrying 'fuel oil'. Would this be a reference to vehicle fuel or domestic heating? Above the tanks in the background is another railway embankment. This once carried the Westerleigh east curve and the train is now approaching what was formerly Westerleigh North Junction. *GH0343*

Image 35: Probably taken from the top of a redundant Junction home signal, we have a view of **BR Standard Class 9F** 2-10-0 92139, coasting onto the north to west curve at the former Westerleigh North Junction. It is in charge of a Class 8 'unfitted through freight' comprised mainly of wagons loaded with both 'lump' and 'pulverised' coal. '92139' is carrying a Saltley (21A) shed plate. It was sent there new from Crewe Works on 31st July 1957 staying until it was moved north late in 1966. It still looks relatively new in this picture. Note the huge lumps of coal piled on its tender. The 107 milepost to the extreme right is of Great Western origin, the distance being taken from Paddington. It marks the exact point of Westerleigh North Junction where the East Curve met with the West Curve. The connecting points are still in place as are the weed grown tracks. Historically this curve was little used and closed on 10th July 1927. However it was reopened on 16th August 1942 as an emergency alternative route during World War 2, but finally taken out of use on 4th January 1950. However from the evidence of this picture – post 1957 – it would appear to have been moth-balled rather than de-commissioned with point rodding and rails still in situ. *GH1319*

Image 36: About a quarter of a mile further on the 'Up' and 'Down' lines of the Westerleigh loop divided. The 'Up' line, straight ahead in this picture, ran across a bridge carrying it over the LMR Main line on a 'flyover', before meeting it at Yate South Junction. At Yate South the 'Down' line struck off onto the 'Down' Westerleigh Curve and the two came together near an area called Rodford. Here George captured a Riddles designed **BR Standard** 'Class 5' 73091 carrying a 'Class 4' headlamp code coasting into the curve with a 'fully fitted freight'. Only close scrutiny can decipher the locomotive's number. This was one of the locomotives sent to Gloucester (Barnwood) (85C) from Shrewsbury in exchange for the six 'Jubilees' exiled from Barrow Road (22A) in August 1961 (See Image 28). Robert Riddles was the first Chief Mechanical Engineer of the nationalised British Railways and his design for a mixed traffic locomotive leant very heavily on that of his mentor William Stanier and his earlier design of the ubiquitous ex-LMS 'Black Five' Class. '73091' was out-shopped from Derby during October 1955. It was based at Gloucester, first Barnwood (85C) until that shed's closure in 1964 and then Horton Road (85B), from where it was withdrawn in May the following year. This would have been its regular stamping ground. It was scrapped at Birds Yard, Risca in South Wales during August 1965, just less than ten years after it was built. *GH0715*

Image 37: Slightly north of the previous image 36 an ex-GWR Hawksworth designed 'Modified Hall' 7925 'Westol Hall' travels south on the single line 'Down' section of Westerleigh Loop at the head of a Class 'D' or a Class '5' freight, depending upon when this picture was taken. As explained earlier in Image 11 the headlamp classifications were changed in July 1962. Prior to this date a Class 'D' was an "express freight, livestock, perishable or ballast train with not less than one-third vacuum braked vehicles piped to the engine". After that date the same headlamp code became a Class '5' with subtle changes to the description, an "express freight train with the automatic brake operative on not less than half of the vehicles". This description eliminated the livestock, perishable element of the train. 'Westol Hall' was delivered from Swindon post-nationalisation on 9th October 1950. She went straight to the West Country and spent her first ten years at Penzance (83G). Then moving to Cardiff in October 1959, she spent most of the rest of her service in South Wales until October 1965 when sent to Oxford (81F). So what is she doing on this route? Well it could be that she was working home to Cardiff via Stoke Gifford. It is an evening shot with shadows of the bush in the left foreground lengthening, so it could be a late summer view. As a possible explanation, in the freight train WTT for 1960 the 1.00pm Bordesley-Stoke Gifford would be passing this point at about 6.40pm. This assumes that 'Westol Hall' would have worked a train from Cardiff to Birmingham before picking up this duty for the return home. Pure conjecture of course! *GH1430*

Image 38: We have now arrived at Yate South Junction and in this photograph, probably taken from the Signal Box, an ex-LMS Hughes 'Crab' 42827 takes the southbound loop line. We have here a very clear view of the northern end of the Westerleigh loop. In the distance the South Junction advanced starter gives the train clearance into the next section but beneath it the Westerleigh Junction distant signal indicates it does not as yet have clearance through the junction. Beyond the signal is the 'flyover' bridge shown in Image 103. The driver looks back inquisitively realising he is now part of the picture. There is no indication as to what Class of train this could be but clearly it is heading for Stoke Gifford Yard rather than Westerleigh. The first wagon behind the tender is a 'Conflat' carrying an early 'British Railways' container. The term 'Conflat' was used to describe a short wheelbase flat wagon designed to carry a container. It was the GWR who coined the term 'Conflat' in their telegraphic coding of railway wagons for containers. Unlike normal wagon loads, containers were only listed to carry furniture or goods unless they were refrigerated containers. British Railways used several standard types of wagon. The Conflat 'A', which could carry one type 'B', or two type 'A' containers, was the most common. This appears to be a Conflat 'A' carrying a type 'B' container. With this vehicle in the consist would probably make this train an express freight. '42827' entered service from Horwich Works in November 1929 carrying the LMS number '13127'. This was revised by the LMS in 1934/5 during a locomotive renumbering scheme to '2827' and from January 1950, to '42827'. From as early as April 1947 it was noted as being allocated to Saltley (21A) and remained there until June 1964. The probability, therefore, is that this would likely be a Washwood Heath to Stoke Gifford freight. *GH802*

Image 39: We now have to retrace our steps right back into Bristol in order to pick up the LMR main line out of the city. Curving round from Midland Junction the first Midland line signal box approached from Temple Meads was Engine Shed Sidings, a typical Ex-Midland style small box controlling access to and from Barrow Road shed. A rather bedraggled 'Castle' opens up past the Box at the head of the northbound 'The Cornishman'. Close inspection of the photograph reveals part of the smoke number plate to look suspiciously like '4078' and oddly the shed code number '82A' has been chalked on the smoke box door beneath the 'TRN 675' just above where the plate would normally sit. 4078 'Pembroke Castle' was briefly allocated to Bath Road (82A) from November 1958 to July 1959 before being moved on to Stafford Road (84A). She would appear not to have been a well favoured engine. At the time of this photograph she had been in service for thirty five years and was to spend her final three years being shunted between four different sheds before being withdrawn from Llanelly (87F) in July 1962. The leading coach behind the tender is an ex-Great Western coach of Charles Collett design which came to be known as 'High Waisters'. The rest of the consist seems to be BR Mark 1's, but all appear to be in the chocolate and cream livery. On the right a small Ivatt tank engine awaits release from the sidings back onto the shed.
GH1500

Image 40: From a similar viewpoint George has captured a 'Black Five' 44851, storming around the bend at the head of an express. Sporting a Derby (17A) shed code this train would probably be destined for York or Newcastle. '44851' was at Derby between October 1955 and September 1962. Alongside the train, seemingly having just deposited some coaches in the sidings, sits a 'Fowler 4F' 43926, a locomotive employed more locally. It was shedded at Barrow Road (22A) from March 1948 right through to its withdrawal in July 1959. On the evidence of the photograph the firemen of both engines have been doing their job efficiently with both locomotives having steam to spare. In the case of the express engine this would be much needed on the three miles climb to Fishponds in front of the train, with a 1 in 63 ruling gradient. In this picture there is a much clearer view of the small Engine Shed Sidings Signal Box, the first Midland designed box on the London Midland route out of the city. As its name implies its raison d'etre was to control the access and egress of Barrow Road shed. Behind the box is the Midland Region Barton Hill Wagon Repair Shops with some of the paraphernalia required for its tasks on show. The signal box also controlled its access from the 'Down' line. Beyond the water tower the Western Region Carriage Sidings can be glimpsed. *GH1496*

Image 41: No more than a couple of hundred yards further on we have another shot of a Western Region train, 'The Cornishman', adjacent to Barrow Road shed. In 1952, with increasing passenger traffic between the West Midlands and the South West the Western Region introduced this express. 'The Cornishman' left Penzance daily at 10.30am (Except Sundays), collecting a portion from Kingswear at Exeter (St. David's). From the evidence of what can be seen of the smoke box number plate on the 'Castle Class' engine in charge, this would probably be 4082 'Dunraven Castle' based at Stafford Road (84A), working home on the final leg of the train's journey to Wolverhampton (Low Level). On its way it passes a Midland '3 Cylinder Compound' 4-4-0 '41144', waiting to come off shed with another locomotive in tow. But why did a Western Region train use the Midland route out of Bristol? We have previously seen 'The Devonian' taking the Western Region route (See Image 20) and the principal reason appears to be an entirely practical one. Beyond Yate South Junction 'The Devonian' and this train shared the same tracks north to Lansdown Junction at Cheltenham. The respective train crews were required to maintain route knowledge and signalling of each other's route out of Bristol. To meet the requirement, in the event of alternative route working when one or other route became unavailable, this was a regular practice. *GH1488*

Image 42: Looking north from the bridge featured in the background of Image 41 we have another view of the holding sidings at Barrow Road shed and on the main line, a 'Black Five' begins the climb to Fishponds. It must be an express bound for Birmingham or beyond which is made up with a rake of ex-LMS coaching stock. The first two behind the tender and the last are still in the 'Crimson Lake' livery of the LMS whereas the ones in between are carrying the 'Crimson and Cream' livery which BR introduced for corridor stock from 1949 and came to be commonly called 'Blood and Custard'. In the yard a Fowler 4F waits to come off shed after the passage of the express, this to be followed by a Midland Compound beyond. Meanwhile in the sidings are four other Midland 4F's. The most visible of these is '44096', displaying a 71G shed code. Between 1950 and 31st January, 1958 this was the code for Bath (Green Park) S & D shed, before being changed to 82F, with the Bath and S & D area being transferred to the Western Region as a result of inter-regional boundary changes. In the siding on the left stands a BR Standard 9F '92134', in light steam. This engine was sent new from Crewe Works to Saltley (21A) on 30th June 1957 before moving to the East Midlands six months later. It may well have brought a freight 'Down' from Birmingham and is now awaiting its return working. From this evidence we may then deduce the picture was taken during the second half of 1957. Note the coaling tower dominating the background. *GH1489*

Image 43: Evening at Barrow Road, capturing all the atmosphere of a steam shed during the 1950's and probably for a century beforehand. The photograph is taken from the road bridge that spanned the site and reveals a splendid variety of locomotives. Taking water on the left, looks most likely to be an ex-Midland Railway 'Class 4F' 0-6-0 originally designed by Henry Fowler in 1911. In 1925 Henry Fowler became the Chief Mechanical Engineer of the LMS, following George Hughes. Very soon afterwards he introduced a superheated development of the type, of which 580 were subsequently built. This very ubiquitous Class was long lived; '44264', which appears to be this engine, was based at sheds either at Gloucester or Bristol through from May 1948 to October 1965 when it was finally withdrawn. Beyond; a pair of 'Black Fives', the foremost of which displays a Train Reporting Number, most probably for an 'excursion' or 'special' working ,wait to head off for Temple Meads. In the middle foreground the boiler of 'Jubilee' 45568 'Western Australia' glints in the evening sunshine. This locomotive was a Holbeck (20A) based engine from 1948 through to 1964, so is clearly staying over before working home the next day. Behind her is an unidentified BR 'Standard Class 9' 2-10-0 alongside an ex-GWR Pannier tank. *GH1492*

Image 44: On the other side of the Barrow Road Bridge, spanning the shed yard stood this tall ex-LMS coaling tower. Beneath it George has captured what suspiciously looks like 'Jubilee' 45577 'Bengal' being coaled, just arrived on her home shed having worked a 'Down' 'Devonian' into Bristol. This engine was allocated to Barrow Road (22A) from September 1952 through to 31st August 1962, when she was one of the seven 'Jubilees' exiled to Shrewsbury. From her appearance, this is then probably an early 1960's view. Behind, in the middle background, is an Ivatt 'Class 2MT' '41243', out-shopped new from Crewe Works in October 1949 and going directly to the Somerset and Dorset at Bath (Green Park) (22C). It spent its entire life on the S&D, being withdrawn from Templecombe in July 1965; just prior to the closure of the S & D. It was probably a regular visitor here working the Bath (Green Park) to Temple Meads local services. From 1950 Bath (Green Park) was transferred to the Southern Region and became (71G). This remained the case until 1st February 1958 when the S & D was transferred to the Western Region becoming (82F). Beyond that an ex-LMS 'Jinty' shunts in the Barrow Road Carriage Sidings. Between 1938 and 1944 the LMS, which led the way nationally with improving operational efficiency, began to modernise its motive power depots; a feature of which was the introduction of coaling plants. The main body of the tower here raised coal wagons on the far side of this tower and discharged the contents direct into locomotive tenders. The top of the tower housed the plant's control cabin accessed by the ladders seen in this photograph. *GH1497*

Image 45: In fact Barrow road was such a busy shed that it had two coaling towers, as seen in this photograph taken from the same bridge. But this is an enchanting picture of still unspoilt, turn of the 1950/60's decade life. In this view another 'Ivatt 2MT' 41284 is in charge of an Empty Coaching Stock (ECS) working past Lawrence Hill Jnc. Signal Box in the background. This Box controlled access and egress to Barrow Road Carriage sidings and the old Midland Railway terminus of St. Philips. The evidence from the very grubby, barely visible, raised home signal alongside the third coach and the fireman looking back towards it, suggests it is assisting a train up the gradient to the junction before dropping the stock into the sidings at the back of the shed. Lawrence Hill Junction marked the beginning of the route on to Temple Meads. '41284', the engine at the head of this train, also went new from Crewe Works to Bath (Green Park), then designated (22C) in September 1949. Here it is carrying a (71G) shed code plate. On a head shunt in the shed yard reclines '47678', a Henry Fowler designed Class 3F 0-6-0T shunting engine; a Barrow Road resident throughout the decade. Another ex-Midland 4F 0-6-0 is beneath the nearest coaling tower. On the other side of the tracks, oblivious to the railway activities, three young girls play around the 'Maypole' whilst two older ones sit quietly in the corner of the playground discussing more serious teenage issues. *GH1494*

Image 46: Immediately west of Barrow Road shed stood the Midland Region carriage sidings. This view records the yard, dominated by ex-LMS coaching stock, except for the rake of BR Mark 1's in the centre which carries 'Newcastle-Bristol' carriage headboards. A Class 3F '47552' 'Jinty' fusses about its duties in the centre; the origin of why this Class came to be given this name remains a mystery. It was a Barrow Road based engine from January 1953 to October 1959. 417 of the Class were built; this one came into service in January 1928 having been built by the Hunslet Engineering Company at Leeds. The three engines on shed beyond the coaches are all Ex-Midland Class 4F's and what looks like the tender of a 'Black Five' is beyond. Tracks in the right foreground led down to St. Philips opened by the Midland Railway in 1870, where an extensive goods yard and small passenger terminus was opened to relieve pressure on Temple Meads. The station had a single platform and was used principally by the local services between Bristol and Bath (Green Park), via Mangotsfield. The Goods Station was renamed Midland Road on 15th September 1952. The local passenger trains were re-routed into Temple Meads and the passenger station closed on 21st September 1953. Midland Road goods station closed on 1st April 1967. *GH1499*

Image 47: Three miles from Temple Meads we come to the first suburban station, Fishponds. From Lawrence Hill Junction trains faced a very stiff climb with a ruling gradient of 1 in 63 before easing to 1in 583 through the station. George has positioned himself at the western end of the 'Down' platform to record a spruce looking 'Jubilee 45608 'Gibraltar' still working hard to get her express over the summit and begin to build some speed. In the still air of a summer day her almost clear exhaust rises vertically into the sky. She is carrying a Train Reporting Number (TRN) 'M214'. The use of a letter in the code was introduced in June 1960 at the start of the summer timetable and was the first stage in introducing a nationwide train reporting numbering system, so we may assume this was when this picture was taken. In this case the letter 'M' indicated that the train was destined for the London Midland Region, inferring it was probably a summer extra, originating its journey on the Western Region, now returning holiday makers home. The locomotive's shed code plate (55A) was Leeds (Holbeck) which gives an indication of where its destination may have been. Originally Holbeck was a Midland Region shed but was renumbered on 1st February 1957 as a result of boundary changes. 'Gibraltar' spent fifteen years based at Holbeck until 1st September 1965 when she was withdrawn and later scrapped.
*GH1449*

Image 48: From the same position, this time from rail level, we have an imposing view of BR 'Class 9F' 2-10-0 92028, one of ten of the class originally fitted with a 'Franco - Crosti' boiler. This boiler was a modification of the conventional fire tube boiler design used on most steam locomotives. Unlike these; the heat remaining in the exhaust gases was used to preheat the water supply for the main boiler using a secondary heat exchange mechanism, thereby using the steam more efficiently. Designed in the very early 1930s by Attilio Franco and Dr Piero Crosti the design came into widespread use across Europe during the following decades. BR was very late on the scene with this experiment in the last years of steam. '92028' was built at Crewe Works and delivered into service in July 1955. Its shed code plate shows a single number and letter suggesting this as being (2E), the code for Saltley (21A) during 1964/65, which helps dating of the photograph. The headlamp code displayed is for a 'Class 8' train; an unfitted through freight. Fascinatingly the figure '8' has been chalked just above the buffer beam to the left. The rake of steel bodied mineral wagons is probably bound for the West Midlands. From the empty Fishponds goods yard seen in the previous Image 47 it now appears to be full of scrap metal. The siding leading into the picture on the left was constructed in 1905 for the Avonside Locomotive Works, to move their newly built locomotives onto the main line. The Company was badly affected by the 1930's Great Depression and went into voluntary liquidation in November 1934. The Fishponds plant and buildings were sold off in 1935 and the goodwill, drawings and patterns were purchased by the Hunslet Engine Company. *GH1448*

Image 49: Clearly it wasn't only 'The Cornishman' that used the Midland route out of Bristol. In this picture George captured a 'Modified Hall' 7907 'Hart Hall' wheezing towards the summit of the two mile climb from Lawrence Hill with a northbound express, the leading two coaches being of ex-LMS coaching stock. Similarly to 'North Aston Hall' in Image 15, 'Hart Hall' was not delivered into service until post-nationalisation, in her case on 5th January 1950. Is the train she has charge of a regular working, a summer extra or a diverted service? There is no indication which would help to identify it. If this picture, in the same sequence as the previous two, was taken around the same time then we would likely be looking at a photograph taken in the early 1960's. During this period 'Hart Hall' was based in Bristol, first at St. Philip's Marsh, from February 1962 to June 1964 and thereafter at Barrow Road (82E); until she was withdrawn on 31st December 1965, subsequent upon the closure of Barrow Road shed. With the locomotive being in far from healthy condition the conclusion has to be that it was during this period that the photograph was taken. Was the engine taking its train all the way through to Birmingham or might it just have made it to Gloucester? She ended life at Cashmore's in Newport, being cut-up during May 1965. *GH1450*

Image 50: Just less than three-quarters of a mile further on was another small suburban station, Staple Hill, set in a cutting at the summit of the climb. The main station building here was on street level; a zigzag path and a footbridge connecting the two platforms with small buildings on each. Note in the background the lattice-framed station footbridge painted half white on the 'Down' side. It is likely this would have been for signal sighting purposes for drivers of trains emerging from the tunnel. In the foreground, shaded by early morning sunshine, a 'lengthman' has parked his bicycle and lit a fire outside his bothy. A rather bedraggled BR Standard Class 5 approaches the tunnel mouth, above which George has positioned himself, with an 'Up' express. A good local service was provided, both here at Staple Hill and Fishponds, by regular trains between Bath (Green Park) also Temple Meads and Gloucester and Temple Meads. As previously stated the service from Bath originally ran into a terminus at St. Philip's. That station was sited close to the Old Market shopping area and also attracted flourishing commuter traffic. This area was badly bombed during World War II, and Bristol's shopping district was rebuilt elsewhere. This, together with the transfer of traffic from St. Philip's to Temple Meads led to a decline in traffic. Even so, as late as 1963, a combined weekday service of nineteen trains plus two (SO), ran to Temple Meads. In the 'Up' direction eighteen, plus four (SO), ran out terminating at Gloucester, Yate, Mangotsfield or Bath. But it didn't last much longer; stopping train services between Bristol and Gloucester were withdrawn from 4th January 1965 and those between Bristol and Bath (Green Park) from 7th March 1966. Staple Hill station was closed at the same time. *GH0719*

Image 51: And so to Mangotsfield, where we see 'Jubilee' 45626 'Seychelles' coasting into the curve through the station with another summer 'extra'. This time the 'TRN' is 'M229', so heading for somewhere on the London Midland Region. George has taken up a position on the 'Down' side just west of Mangotsfield Station Signal Box. The raised 'home' signal indicates she has 'got the road' through the station but the Mangotsfield North Junction distance signal remains at caution, thus restricting her approach. The train is made up of mixed coaching stock which by then was twenty five to thirty years old and being used for 'excursions' or summer 'extras' such as this. The first three coaches are of an ex-LMS design with the one in the middle looking like a Period 1 coach dating to the late 1920's. Throughout the 1950's decade 'Seychelles' was based at Derby (17A) from June 1951 through to December 1961 when she went to Burton (17B) until November 1962. So with Train Reporting Numbers (TRN) being introduced for the summer timetable in 1960 and 'Seychelles' being based at Derby until December 1961, we may deduce this picture would have been taken during the summers of either 1961 or 1962. Finally '45626' was noted as being in the Erecting Shop at Crewe Works on the 1st April 1964, by which time she had been allocated to Holbeck. Was this her swansong overhaul perhaps? She was withdrawn eighteen months later on 11th October 1965. *GH0818*

Image 52: From virtually the same position George has now turned around to record the 'Down' 'Devonian' sweeping through Mangotsfield on its approach into Bristol. With a cloudless sky and short shadows it appears to be a warm summer day. The 'Jubilee' 45573 'Newfoundland' was based at Leeds (Holbeck) (20A) right through from the day BR was formed on 1st January 1948 until she was withdrawn on 1st September 1965. She looks to be very well turned out. The first corporate crest for locomotives was introduced in 1949 and was the 'Lion on Wheel 'emblem which 'Newfoundland' carries, on the tender, in this picture. Essentially Mangotsfield was an outer suburban station; indeed some services into Bristol started and terminated here. Close scrutiny of the picture reveals a sign on the platform 'The Devonian' is running through, directing passengers to an opposite platform for Bristol St. Philips which closed on 21st September 1953 (See Image 46). From this information we may deduce the photograph would have been taken in the first years of the 1950's. As can be seen Mangotsfield was quite an expansive junction station with extensive glass canopies. This was a 'new' station built by the Midland Railway at the time of the opening of the Bath to Bristol line on 4th August 1869. Replacing the original station at Mangotsfield North Junction, it was built on the southern face of Rodway Hill, having three island platforms, giving six platform faces, with the junction apex forming the western end of the middle island as seen in this picture. Mangotsfield closed on 7th March 1966 alongside the withdrawal of the Green Park to Bristol passenger service. Finally; just note the fire fighting arrangements such as they were; three red buckets filled with water or sand, hanging on the signal box wall! *GH0837*

Image 53: Another dreamy summer day with cotton wool clouds breaking up the blue sky. George is once again in the same position, this time to capture an ex-GWR 'Castle' Class engine heading what we might assume to be another summer 'extra,' carrying holiday makers to the south-west. Alas we are not able to identify the locomotive but it is safe to say she was due a visit to Swindon! The intriguing feature is the 'TRN 825 'displayed on the smoke box door. From the summer timetable 1952, possibly earlier, this referred to the Western Region 9.00am (SX) Wolverhampton to Penzance. This number had the same designation throughout the decade until the summer of 1958. Such was the passenger traffic between the West Midlands and Devon and Cornwall during the middle of the decade, this train ran all the year round. For the summer timetable in 1952, British Railways introduced the title 'The Cornishman' for this cross-country express. So, could this be a picture taken before the introduction of 'The Cornishman' headboard, prior to the Summer 1952 timetable? In 1961, the train was still using Wolverhampton Low Level, for the down service, starting at 9.00am, running along the original Great Western route via Stratford- upon-Avon through Cheltenham and Gloucester at 11:02am and 11:20am respectively. From Bristol, at 12:15, it arrived Plymouth at 3:15pm and finally, Penzance at 5:55pm. As we saw earlier there was a reciprocal arrangement between the Western Region and the London Midland Region so 'The Cornishman' was a regular on the south end of the Midland route into Bristol. With the train consist being of BR Mark 1 coaches, and without the engine carrying a headboard this could be a mid to late 1950's view. *GH0829*

Image 54: **A late autumn or winter evening at Mangotsfield and if the evidence from the carriage headboard is to be believed we are looking at a Newcastle to Bristol express. As seen earlier (Images 03 and 15) George became one of the earliest exponents of night-time railway photography. This is a time-exposure shot requiring everything to remain still whilst the camera is given time to absorb the available light. As here the result could be quite stunning; emphasising the light emanating from the engine's fire. For this view he stood on the southern flank of Rodway Hill to get a bird's eye view of BR 'Standard Class 5' 73003 and its train standing in the main 'Down' Platform. The other lines beyond are those from Bath coming in from the left. Note the contrast between the warm glow of the lights in the signal box and those of the glaring glow and heat of the footplate. To be able to successfully capture these contrasts would take a good degree of judgement with the camera's exposure setting and shutter speed; no mean feat. '73003' had been re-allocated to Barrow Hill shed in January 1958. A week or so later on 1st February 1958, due to boundary changes, Barrow Hill was re-designated (82F), a code this locomotive would have carried on its smoke box shed plate. With reference to the Western Region Working Timetable for the period 12th September, 1960 to 11th June 1961 the weekday 12.43pm ex-Newcastle to Bristol stood at Mangotsfield from 8.5pm to 8.9pm (9 minutes later on Saturdays). Given Mangotsfield was a junction station the only reason for this could have been to provide a connection to Bath; the four minutes indicating sufficient time for the transfer of mail, perhaps. The 8.10pm from Temple Meads was the last 'down' train of the day from Temple Meads to Bath which was due at Mangotsfield at 8.26pm and away at 8.31pm; allowing sufficient time for the transfer to be completed.** *GH0821*

Image 55: Mangotsfield Station was set at the western point of a triangle of lines, the west to south side carrying the line to Bath (Green Park). Here George is at Mangotsfield South Junction as an' Ivatt Class 2' 2-6-2 tank engine, running bunker first, runs onto the lines to Bath at the point where they meet those of the eastern curve from Mangotsfield North. During autumn 1949 Green Park (22C) received four of these Ivatt engines new from Crewe Works. '41240-43' then spent the next decade becoming the staple locomotives on this service, with other members of the Class being transferred in later. During the early years, in the summers of the 1950's, there was quite an intensive service operating between Bristol and Bath; fourteen trains on weekdays and fifteen on Saturdays. Four of these ran from Temple Meads, two of which were through trains to Bournemouth, and the other ten ran from St. Philip's. In the opposite direction, on weekdays, there were two to Temple Meads and thirteen into St. Philip's with one extra train to Temple Meads on a Saturday. Prior to WWll St. Philip's station had been much more conveniently placed for Bristol's Market, shops and business centre. But the Old Market area was badly bombed during the war and Bristol's shopping district was rebuilt elsewhere. As a result there was a substantial decline in passenger traffic which led to closure of St. Philip's on 21st September 1953 and the transfer of local passenger trains into Temple Meads. The decline continued and the Bristol-Bath service was finally withdrawn on the 7th March 1966, coinciding with the closure of the S & D. *GH2189*

Top Image 56: Moving on to Bath and specifically; the Somerset and Dorset line between Bath Junction and Devonshire Tunnel. Photographed in the early years of the decade we see an 'Up' S& D train with the pilot engine curiously displaying a 'Class F' (express freight train) headlamp code. So what may be the explanation? This was a time when the S & D was still operating full blast and a far cry from ten years hence. The two ex-Midland 'Class 2P' (Compound) 4-4-0 engines descend from Devonshire Tunnel in full steam with what appears to be a rake of Richard Maunsell designed ex-Southern Railway coaches. The safety valves on each engine are just feathering steam but their regulators are still open on a falling gradient! The pilot engine, with its fireman casually leaning over the cab side, is '40698', a longstanding Green Park (22C) engine from the 1940's right through until July 1960, when it was withdrawn. Although it cannot be definitively stated, the train engine looks suspiciously like '40601', which was also a long term Green Park (22C) engine before being withdrawn in December 1959. As for a train of this length, it would probably be a working from Bournemouth West or Templecombe, picking up the pilot engine at Evercreech Junction. The headlamp code of the pilot may have referred to the train it worked 'Down' with to Evercreech. *GH1375*

Bottom Image 57: We are still in the same area but George has now moved over to the other side of the tracks and taken up a position on the rising ground. From this viewpoint he captures a Bournemouth bound summer express in the hands of what is probably one of Green Park's 'Black Fives' piloted by 'Compound' No. 40634. The latter engine was based at Templecombe (22D) from Nationalisation Day on 1st January 1948 and probably earlier, right through until May 1962 when it was withdrawn from service. Clearly one of its principal duties was piloting between Evercreech Junction and Bath (Green Park). This climb out of Bath with a ruling gradient of 1 in 50 all the way up to the mouth of Combe Down Tunnel, including the passage through Devonshire Tunnel, was the first challenge of what was to come. Piloting duties provided long term work for a number of locomotives and footplate crews at Templecombe until the introduction of BR 'Standard Class 9' engines in 1960. The 'Black Fives were introduced on a trial basis to the S&D during 1938 when still in LMS days, '5440' was allocated to Bath (Green Park). Very soon, amongst engine crews and shed staff, they became the most popular engines ever to run on the S&D. Note that the pilot is carrying the same headlamp code as the pilot engine in Image 56. *GH1402*

Image 58: Two young enthusiasts cling to one of the strands of the wire fence to watch the trains go by. And they are rewarded as a 'Black Five' 44917 storms the 1 in 50 gradient towards Devonshire Tunnel. The safety valves are lifting, so the fireman having prepared his fire well has time to lean out of the cab and take in a lungful of air before the train plunges into Devonshire and Combe Down Tunnels. The engine is in charge of a rake of eight coaches, likely to be a through train from the north to Bournemouth, which it is going to haul up to Masbury Summit unaided. One would expect to see an express headlamp code displayed but confusingly the one carried is yet again a 'Class F' (Express freight not fitted with continuous brakes). Was this a headlamp code peculiar to the S&D? This is undoubtedly an early decade photograph; note the post-war 'prefabs' built at the bottom of the embankment to the left. From March, 1952 until June 1958 '44917' was one of the 'Black Fives' allocated to Green Park (By then 71G) for working over the S&D. Their successful use ultimately led to the introduction of 'BR Standard Class 5's on the route to continue their success. (See Image 167) *GH1377*

Image 59: Moving back to Mangotsfield we are now at the opposite end of the station and, from a 'Down' side vantage point, looking at a Birmingham bound express leaving Mangotsfield on the west to north curve leading to Westerleigh North Junction. Rodway Hill is now to our right. From the long shadows the rising sun is in the east and with shrubs in bloom in the background we may infer this shot was perhaps taken in early autumn possibly featuring either the 7.40am or 8.40am from Temple Meads, both of which called at Mangotsfield. The engine in charge is a 'Caprotti' fitted 'Black Five' 44747. She looks very well maintained; obviously in regular use on passenger traffic. Its shed plate shows it is a Barrow Road (22A) allocated engine. It was based at Bristol for eight years from 1949 to 1957 so this is a view from the first half of the 1950's. The Caprotti valve gear was a type invented in the early 1920s by Italian engineer and architect Arturo Caprotti. Unlike piston valve types, the Caprotti type consisted of poppet valves, rotary camshafts, and closed mechanisms, intended to lead to less wear and tear, and more effective steam distribution to the inside cylinder, all of which made for better efficiency. There are two interesting features in the picture; the house and the clerestory carriage in the foreground. The ornate bargeboards on the house behind the engine suggests it may be a railway house and with its direct access to the station looks substantial enough to have been the Station Master's, built by the Midland Railway. As for the ancient coach in the foreground; the same vehicle was seen behind the signal box in Image 54. It appears to be an ex-GWR Clerestory coach dating back to the late Victorian era, now in Departmental use for stores or as a 'Mess Coach' on Permanent Way or Engineering trains. *GH0834*

Image 60: Some six to eight years later and taken from virtually the same viewpoint as in the previous photograph, this picture looks to have been taken on a sunny late winter/early spring afternoon. Note how the shadow cast by the telegraph pole has changed. This could be around Easter time; the first holiday surge of the year. The train engine, 'Black Five' 45447 has had its smoke box cleaned to proudly head 'The Devonian'. By this time the train was due to leave Temple Meads at 12.40pm and the shadows of the hedge and telegraph poles reinforce the view that this may be springtime. The fact that it is a heavy train is indicated by it being double-headed, unusually, by a steam engine and a diesel. The pilot engine is a 'Peak' Class locomotive, the number of which cannot be discerned. The 'Peaks' (BR Sulzer Type 4) began to be introduced from August 1959 and rapidly began to displace engines such as the 'Jubilees' and 'Black Fives' on the Midland main line between Bristol and the north. '45447' was allocated to Saltley (21A) from November 1959 until June 1965. This was at a time when steam was very much being run down at Bristol and indeed Barrow Road was the last steam shed to close in the city on 20th November 1965. The presentation of the 'Peak' indicates it has already lost its first flush of youth. The train has just coasted through the station; a speed restriction of 30mph was placed on the Mangotsfield Station to North Junction curve. Note the siding seen in the foreground of Image 59 has also now disappeared; even the bargeboards on the house are in need of repainting! With these observations it would suggest this picture would have likely been taken during the late first half of the 1960's. *GH0836*

Image 61: We now have a view of one of those diesels taking its leave of Mangotsfield with 'TRN 1N21' on an English late summer day. All the vegetation is in full flower and growth and the sky is calm. It has not been possible to establish the exact train to which this code applied but it was in consequence of the introduction of national Train Reporting Numbers from 1962. The letter 'N' indicated that the train was bound for the North Eastern Region. The signal the engine is passing is the Mangotsfield North Junction 'outer home' and the other in the background is a similar signal protecting the approach from Bath on the south to north curve. This 'Peak' diesel 'D138' appears to be in pristine condition. It was introduced into service from Derby Works on 21st October 1961 and initially sent to Derby (17A). After a short period it was re-allocated to Carlisle Upperby (12B) but returned to Derby in May 1962 and remained there until September 1964. This information together with the engine's condition suggests this picture perhaps being taken during the summer of 1962 with a working which it would have taken from Bristol through to Derby. The shadow of the bush in the foreground indicates the sun is still high but moving to the south-west. If that is the case this train could be the 4.35pm departure from BTM, 'The Cornishman'. From 10th September 1962 "The Cornishman" was diverted from its original route to the Midland line via the Lickey. At the same time its northerly destination was changed from Wolverhampton (Low Level) to Sheffield (Midland), hence the introduction of the 'Peak' diesels to this train. *GH0826*

Image 62: This view looks very much as though it was taken from Mangotsfield North Junction Signal Box. It shows a pair of 'Peak Class' diesels a couple of hundred yards on from the previous location. Again the 'TRN 1N37' was a newly introduced four digit code for the 1962 summer timetable and the full number of the pilot engine cannot be fully distinguished other than the final number, being a '2'. A large proportion of these engines went straight to Derby (17A) when they were released into service and the likelihood is these would be two of them. In the background rises Rodway Hill the southern flank of which was excavated to accommodate Mangotsfield station. Opposite, built within the triangle of lines, is a good view of Carson's Chocolate Factory. To the right, in sidings used for stabling coaches, an ancient carriage has taken up residence against the wooden stop block; no doubt awaiting its final journey. The metal mineral wagons are loaded with pulverised coal probably awaiting delivery to a power station or other industrial facility. Beyond the first wagon the keen eyed may spot a railwayman cycling along from the station. Perhaps he is the relief for the present signalman on duty. *GH0831*

Image 63: This superb view of Mangotsfield North Junction, absolutely encapsulates the railway scene during the 1950's. The substantial buildings on the left are those of the original Mangotsfield Station of 1845 placed much nearer to Shortwood village than Mangotsfield itself. The Bristol and Gloucester Railway opened in 1844 to run services between Bristol and Gloucester. Engineered on the 7 ft (2.134 m) Broad Gauge, it was acquired in 1845 by the 4 ft 8 1/2 in (1.435 m) standard gauge Birmingham and Gloucester Railway which was acquired by the Midland Railway, at the same time. On a lovely summer morning this picture records one of Fowler's ubiquitous 'Class 4F's' 44523 running off the Westerleigh South Junction to Westerleigh North Junction chord at the head of a 'Class H' (unfitted through freight). This east chord line opened in 1873 and formed a triangle at Mangotsfield, enabling trains to run direct between Bath and Gloucester. This was followed on the 20th July 1874 by the opening of the Somerset and Dorset northern extension across the Mendips. The S & D allied itself with the Midland Railway using that Company's passenger station and goods facilities at Bath. The East chord then came into its own and for many years carried heavy summer holiday traffic from the Midlands to Bournemouth. Not least of this was the 'Pines Express'. '44523' was a long term resident of Bath (Green Park) (22C), spending the majority of its life on this route and that of the Somerset and Dorset. In this case the 'goods' train was probably bound from Bath to Westerleigh Yard where it would be re-sorted. As can be seen, the sidings on the right were used for the storage of passenger coaches not in continuous use, but would be available for excursion or other extra trains as required. *GH823*

Image 64: Probably taken on the same morning and from a similar viewpoint this picture records a 'Jubilee' 45577 'Bengal' sweeping out of the west to north curve past Mangotsfield North Junction signal box at the head of a Bristol to Birmingham express. With the regulator open she begins to accelerate for the relatively easy road ahead. 'Bengal' was built in Glasgow by the North British Locomotive Company and delivered into service on 29th September 1934. She spent the first eighteen years of her life working across the Scottish border between Carlisle and Glasgow before being transferred to Barrow Road (22A) in September 1952. She looks a little grimy but in good fettle; showing a clean exhaust. The shadows cast indicate the morning sun is still quite low. The timetable of the period shows two likely contenders as to which train this might be; the 7.40am Temple Meads to Bradford or the 8.40am to Sheffield. Both trains called at Mangotsfield to pick up passengers with connections from Bath (See Image 54). The engine's exhaust emphasises the point that she is probably restarting the train after a call. The other feature of the photograph is the prominent building behind the engine. This was Carson's Chocolate Factory, which can also be seen in a number of the preceding images. This factory was built in 1913 in the middle of the triangle with sidings accessed from Mangotsfield North. In 1961 the Shortwood factory was sold due to over capacity and moved to another factory in Bristol. The present reader may be more familiar with 'Elizabeth Shaw' chocolates acquired by the Company in 1968 and still produced to this day. *GH0824*

Image 65: A little further north and the 'silent sentinels' give an unidentified 'Black Five' and its parcels train a clear road ahead. In this view at Mangotsfield North, the old station buildings and the North Junction signal box are obscured by foliage. From the shadows cast this would appear to be another early morning picture. But in this instance George seems to be concentrating less on the train and rather more the focal point; the set of signals. There was always more to railways than just trains! This bracket signal post carries two sets of signals; those to the right are for the road to Bristol whilst the pair on the left is for Bath; but what do they mean? In this instance the upper signal on the right is the North Junction 'home' starter signal which has been cleared for the train to pass into the next section. Below it is the Mangotsfield Station distant signal which means the home signals for the next block section have also been set to 'off', effectively meaning the train has the whole section clear through to the approach to Kingswood Junction. On the left is the 'home' starter for the Bath route via the east curve. The distant signal below it is that for Westerleigh South Junction at the other end of the triangle. On the 'Up' side of the main lines the sidings are still full of stored coaches, some in better repair than others. *GH0830*

Image 66: From morning we move to evening at the same location but have now crossed the tracks to the opposite embankment and moved on in time. The shadows and late sunshine give a dappled effect on the second coach which looks to be relatively deserted. Unusually the train is headed by an unidentified 'Royal Scot' Class 4-6-0 or is it a 'Baby Scot', i.e. a rebuilt 'Patriot' Class 4-6-0? The two BR 'Mark 1' coaches in view suggest this is probably a Bristol bound express although there are no coach headboards to confirm it. The livery of corridor coaching stock was originally trialled by the nascent BR in 'Carmine and White' (nicknamed Plum and Spilt Milk) before 'Crimson Lake and Cream' livery (Blood and Custard) replaced it; being adopted in 1949 across the network. Non-corridor stock was painted plain Crimson Lake. This was replaced in 1956 by the livery these coaches are carrying; an all-over darker maroon which more closely resembled that of the pre-nationalisation LMS. By contrast to the previous image the now overgrown carriage sidings on the 'Up' side are host to just six varied vehicles; some possibly condemned. The four passenger coaches appear to be all ex-LMS whilst the Parcels van looks like a BR MK1 BG Full Brake Van. The most interesting is the foremost which is an LMS 4 Wheel Motor Car Van. 150 of these were built in 1938, with a further 75 by BR in 1952-1957. Although classed as motor car vans, they were also used for parcels and mail. In front of the main train note the coal stacks full to overflowing; not only are the staithes full but so too is the former cattle dock. Lastly notice the barge boards, on what are now the railway houses (and compare with Images 59 & 60); both have ex-Midland Railway hallmarks. *GH0828*

Image 67: A little further on a Caprotti fitted 'Black Five' 44754 storms away past the Mangotsfield North advanced starter at the head of a 'Class C' or 'Class 3/4' ( fully fitted freight which could be scheduled to run in passenger train timings). Train classification codes changed from letters to numerals on 18th June 1962. This headlamp code probably indicates a train of 'perishables', possibly fruit or vegetables from the South-West to the Midlands and quite likely beyond. It could also be carrying dairy products, namely butter, cheese or cream; don't forget, during the period of the photograph, the railways were still the principal carriers of such products. In any event '44754' is keen to get its cargo underway. The engine was delivered new from Crewe Works to Leeds (Holbeck) (20A) on the 4th April 1948 and served out most of its time there until September 1961. This locomotive was another of the Class fitted with 'Caprotti Valve Gear' (see Image 59) but also had the added benefit of 'Timken Roller Bearings'. The Timken Roller Bearing Company was American, founded in 1889 by Henry Timken, a German immigrant who invented an improved bearing for use on passenger coaches and later steam engines. They became widely used in America as a way of reducing friction. In Britain they had originally been used on the' Turbomotive' a modified 'Princess Royal Class' designed by William Stanier, built by the LMS in 1935. It was later rebuilt as a conventional locomotive '46202 Princess Anne'. Subsequently a number of newly built Class Five locomotives were used to further trial their use during the early BR years. The trials must have been partially successful; some of William Stanier's 'Coronation Class' Pacifics, later became retro-fitted with them. GH0839

Overleaf Image 68: We are now at Shortwood; the heart of the village was the Bridge Inn seen on the left. The bridge in the picture is the same as that from which the previous image was taken. The veranda of the pub was clearly a delightful spot from which to see the trains go by; how could one better spend an afternoon? Emerging from beneath the bridge with a northbound express is an ex-LMS, Henry Fowler designed, 'Patriot' Class 4-6-0 45509 'The Derbyshire Yeomanry'. Delivered from Crewe Works in August 1932 she is still carrying out mainline duties but here looking very much in her dotage. Her exhaust displays her condition; in need of some tender loving care. This is a late afternoon/early evening shot; is George telling us the sun is going down on her service? From November 1951 until September 1958 she was based at Derby (17A) so was probably very familiar with this route. Quite possibly, so too was the first vehicle behind the tender of this express. This is a 'Fruit D' van, first introduced by the GWR in 1939 and so named as a result of the Great Western policy of assigning each type of wagon a telegraphic code to enable formations of wagons to be easily communicated by telegraph. These four-wheeled ventilated vans were built with lighting; some gas and later ones electric. Also being fully- braked with standard vacuum braking, they therefore had two features which made the vehicles suitable for conveyance in passenger trains. BR continued to build these functional vans through to 1958. On this route they were no doubt in use carrying fruit and vegetables from the south-west to the midlands and the north. *GH0838*

Above Image 69: Moving further north a 'Class B' passenger train approaches Shortwood Sidings and has just passed that signal box's outer 'home' signal which has already been returned to 'danger'. The 'Jubilee' at its head has a miscellany of vehicles in tow, consisting of two passenger coaches, a 'Fruit D' van then a further four bogie vehicles, also likely to be vans. In the 1958/59 Working Timetable nine weekday 'Up' stopping passenger trains are shown running daily between Bristol and Gloucester; the same number being replicated in the 1960/61 timetable. But by the winter timetable of 1962/63 these had reduced to eight, three of which ran on Saturdays only. Throughout the 1950's/early 1960's one of these, the 6.30pm ex-Temple Meads remained a constant in the timetable, running through to Birmingham (New Street). The atmosphere conveyed by this picture suggests it to be an evening view. If that is the case then this is probably that train. The 'Jubilee' in charge, 45682 ' Trafalgar', was delivered into service from Crewe Works on 6th January 1936 and was first noted as allocated to Bristol (Barrow Road) (22A) at the beginning of November 1947. From then, apart from short loan periods at Trafford Park Manchester (19G), during autumn 1948, and Sheffield (Millhouses) in November, 1957 she spent her entire life at Barrow Road. During this period the conveyance of fruit and vegetables from the south-west continued to provide the railways with income. This plodding train took almost four hours to arrive at Birmingham (New Street), not due there until 10.26pm. It ran via Worcester (Shrub Hill) where it stood for nineteen minutes to enable the Bristol - York Mail to pass it on the Worcester avoiding line. With all the calls this train made it may be assumed that, by the time it arrived at New Street, it was laden with produce for Birmingham Market. *GH0070*

Image 70: Further on, and just before the brickworks, was another crossing carrying a public footpath over the railway. A man with his pedal cycle may just be discerned beside the crossing, waiting for the train to pass. Evident in the background are three chimneys pinpointing the brickworks. Shortwood Brick and Tile Company was established in the late 1800's with the coming of the Midland Railway line. Due to the good quality red clay extracted from a nearby clay pit it was able to produce millions of bricks that were fired for local buildings. It became well known for the strength and attractive appearance of its bricks. The clay pit was connected to the brick works by its own narrow gauge railway. Alas it finally closed in 1969, after the railway which had provided its outlet. With the telegraph posts at this point being on the 'Up' side, this photograph, taken much earlier than the previous image, suggests this Stanier 'Black Five' 44963 is heading south with a twelve coach express of pre-nationalisation stock. If that is right then with the sunlight coming from the east this picture would have been taken in the early morning. As evidenced by its shed code plate the engine was based at Saltley (21A) from December 1954 to April 1964 and prior to that Derby (17A) so is seen here possibly heading an overnight working from Newcastle or Yorkshire. *GH0102*

Image 71: Further north on the other side of Shortwood Sidings another public footpath crossed the railway. This is an area where George and Shirley must have taken their evening strolls. Here George persuaded his wife to sit on the corner of the wooden stile to watch the train go by. In his photographs he often used a member of his family as a means of providing perspective. As in this case the technique also often led the eye into his picture. The introduction of a young lady also adds charm to the atmosphere of an evening stroll across the fields. Note the fireman looking out from the locomotive's cab; has he got his eyes on her or had he spotted the cameraman waiting and taken the opportunity to be in the shot? The ex- Midland Railway design of Shortwood Sidings signal box, which can just be seen in the background, was on the 'Up' side. The bracket signal opposite the box controlled the entrance to the Shortwood Brick and Tile Company sidings. The express, largely composed of BR Mk 1 coaches has just passed the Shortwood 'Home' starter signal and the 'Distant' signal below it is also cleared for a straight run through Westerleigh South Junction. The train engine is a BR 'Standard Class 5' 73015 which was based at Barrow Road (22A) from May 1957 to July 1965 so with this photograph having the appearance of a late 1950's/early 1960's view the inference is, it is heading for Birmingham. *GH1236*

Image 72: A lovely summer day and a fine afternoon for a picnic; where better to have it but in a field beside the railway, watching the trains go by? It recalls memories of far off days when life was more frugal and pleasures much simpler. Trailing a white ribbon of smoke and steam, a smart looking 'Black Five', with its express, skirts the scarp of Pucklechurch Ridge as it coasts steadily along the level stretch towards Shortwood. Pucklechurch Ridge is an area of high ground upon the top of which stands the village from which the ridge takes its name. For just a short distance the western scarp of the ridge provides a theatrical backcloth to the railway. Regarding the locomotive; through a process of elimination and given that this is probably a mid 1950's view; the only possible contender would be '44859'. This engine was based at Saltley (21A) from December 1954 to April 1964. It is carrying a Train Reporting Number on its smoke box door but alas this is illegible. This would have been an inter-regional working probably originating in the Midlands or Yorkshire area. From 1959 the reporting number would have indicated the destination of the train, in this case the Western Region. Historically train reporting numbers were used to denote trains in the internal working timetable. But in BR days these were developed to one or more letters or numbers to either uniquely identify a particular train, or denote its route. *GH0100*

Image 73: George was drawn back to this location more than once and in this view, from much the same place as the previous Image 72, he recorded another well turned-out 'Black Five' 44841 heading south-west with likely the same train on a different occasion. Again we are in high summer with the sky filled with voluminous cotton wool clouds. '44841' was another Saltley (21A) based engine from October 1951 until April 1965; apart from a one month loan to Leicester (G.C.) (19F) during October/November 1958. Although a Mixed Traffic engine, Saltley appears to have been keeping some 'Black Fives' in top condition for passenger express work. It was delivered new from Crewe Works in November 1944, towards the end of World War II and spent all its life working out of Midland sheds. Despite being noted undergoing some kind of overhaul in the Erecting Shop at Crewe Works in January 1965, it was withdrawn from service eighteen months later in October 1966 and was broken-up at Cashmore's Scrap Yard, Great Bridge (Birmingham) four months later. Emulating the GWR, the LMS and later LMR gave some cross country services, excursions and relief trains numerical codes; 'W220' was the 'Down' 'Pines Express'. The number was made up from paper stickers applied to a backing board attached to the top smoke box lamp iron, as seen in this picture. The main purpose of the headcode was to assist the signalman in routing and regulating the train correctly, and it was especially useful if services became disrupted. *GH0149*

Opposite Bottom Image 74: We have now reached Westerleigh Sidings and in particular the north end, certainly where George must have forged a friendship with the signalmen of Westerleigh North Junction signal box and through them other railwaymen, specifically footplate men who worked goods trains in and out of the Yard. Westerleigh Sidings was the Midland route's marshalling yard outside Bristol. Until the final years of the 1950's it was here that many 'Down' goods trains terminated, then having been sorted, the vans and wagons made up other trains for onward journeys to destinations around Bristol, Bath and further afield. Likewise on the 'Up' side trains would arrive from Bristol, Avonmouth, Bath and the S & D to be formed into trains for Gloucester, Birmingham and beyond. In this evening view 'Jubilee' 45651 'Shovell' storms past North Junction box with a northbound evening express whilst the silhouetted signal man with his hand on a lever stands ready to confirm the tail-lamp is displayed on the rear vehicle of the train. 'Shovell' was another of those six 'Jubilees' (see Image 28) expelled from Barrow Road to Shrewsbury on the 31st August 1961 making this a late mid 1950's view. Many a young train spotter in the 1950's learnt a bit of history and geography from their interest in railways. Take the names of the 'Jubilee' Class locomotives, in this case 'Shovell'; how did it come to be so named? A number of the Class took their names from famed naval commanders in British history. Sir Cloudesley Shovell was Admiral of the Fleet in the late 17th/early 18th century. He died in 1707 during a disastrous shipwreck in a storm off the Isles of Scilly as his fleet was returning to England after completing a number of successful campaigns in the Mediterranean. *GH1229*

This Page Image 75: George enjoyed nothing more than the atmosphere generated by an evening shot. Taken from much the same position, a busy scene captures, a 'Black Five' 44966, racing effortlessly through the Yard with a 'Class 4' express freight (pipe fitted throughout with the automatic vacuum brake operative on not less than 90 per cent of the vehicles). Close inspection of the photograph reveals that the 90 per cent is largely made up of four wheeled ventilated vans, the indication being they would likely be carrying fruit or vegetables from the south-west to the midlands. The speed with which the train is travelling fully justifies the description 'express freight'. Meanwhile, approaching the signal box on the loop line is what appears to be a 'Fowler Class 4' engine, running tender first. It is either shunting or bringing another goods up to the bracket mounted starter signal. In the right background more steam can be seen as another engine goes about its task of shunting the Yard. An interesting feature of this picture is the signalling arrangements. To the left of the engine the LMS style bracket signals have been raised giving clearance to a southbound train on the main line. In contrast the signals on the 'Up' side are pure ex- Great Western on wooden posts topped with finials on which the home signal has fallen to allow the express freight to pass. '44966' was introduced into service from Horwich Works in August 1946 going to Saltley (21A). It appears to have spent most of its life passing this way, bouncing between spells at both Saltley and Barrow Road (22A) until September 1964 by which time steam had all but disappeared on the route. It was condemned in September 1966 after twenty years' service, at a time when steam engines were being withdrawn rapidly. *GH1245*

Opposite Top Image 76: 'Jubilee Class' 45696 'Arethusa' speeds through Westerleigh Yard with an excursion or additional holiday train on a busy day in 1960. The train's reporting number is shown as '1X68', in traditional LMR style and this is a heavy train consisting of thirteen ex-LMS built coaches. The shed code plate displayed by '45696' tells us this is an **Aston, Birmingham (3D)** based locomotive. She was only at Aston for four months from February to June 1960, thus providing a very narrow window when this picture could have been taken; the likelihood being late spring or early summer. On the 'Down' side a very long goods train has just arrived in the loop; the brake van is just coming into view. In the distance the engine of this train appears to be a 'Black Five' or a 'Stanier 8F'. Beyond it can be seen the steam from an engine in the 'Up' side yard. The evening shadows cast by the express suggests the goods train may have been the 1.30pm Washwood Heath to Westerleigh freight, which was due at Westerleigh Sidings at 7.28pm after a very protracted six hour journey. This was a 'Class H' 'Through freight not fitted with the automatic brake'. The train would have been broken up and re-sorted here. Throughout her life 'Arethusa' was a much travelled engine spending the early part of the 1950's criss-crossing the Scottish border. In this picture she is matched to an ex-LMS 'Fowler' 3500 gallon tender rather than the more common 'Stanier' design. The name 'Arethusa' was taken from Greek Mythology, another source of inspiration for the naming of 'Jubilee' engines. *GH1235*

Opposite Bottom Image 77: Another busy evening at Westerleigh Sidings as this time  BR 'Standard Class 4' 73137 races through on the 'Up' main, overtaking 'Black Five' 44943 with its likely 'Class C or D' train of 'fish, fruit, vegetables or other perishables', which has been 'put inside' onto the loop in order to allow the express to pass. '73137' is displaying a 17A shed code plate at the bottom of its smoke box door. Records show it was only allocated to Derby (17A) for ten months from January 1959 to November the same year, which accurately dates this photograph. The trees are still bare but the bushes indicate some growth which suggests late spring. The bracket signal casts an evening shadow across the rails. In the relevant Working Timetable for 1959 the only express this could be would have been the 7.25pm Temple Meads to Newcastle passenger and postal. Because of the 'punctuality' requirement of the Post Office this train would be given preference all along the route; hence the freight being in the loop. A 'Class C' train would run to the same timing schedule as a passenger train and usually consist of mostly bogie vehicles. This van train has given preference to the express so is more likely to be a 'Class D' express freight of four wheeled vans possibly carrying fruit or vegetables. '73137' would probably have taken the postal all the way through to Derby before being relieved by a Holbeck engine. Interestingly '44943' was sent newly built from Horwich Works to Holbeck in December 1946 and operated out of there until September 1963. This may give some indication as to where the freight train was bound. *GH1220*

This page Image 78: In this picture we are looking at the locomotive crew of the train waiting in the loop in the previous Image 77. As was stated earlier George befriended railwaymen; here to the point of persuading them to abandon the footplate to be photographed beside their steed at the head of the freight train. As a crew in charge of a freight train there was always the occupational hazard of having to wait for more important trains to pass. This photograph illustrates a case in point. Away from the footplate, which they

may be going to share for the next few hours whilst each are engaged in their individual duties, the crew take time out for a chat, one to explain, one to learn, perhaps. The interesting feature is the age difference between the two men: The driver, on the right, is perhaps the wrong side of sixty whilst the fireman on the left is thirty to forty years of age. Is the fireman picking his brains? This photograph fully illustrates the railways philosophy of promotion by seniority. In their own time each man would have begun their careers in their teenage years doing the dirty job on the shed as a humble engine cleaner. From there they advanced to the role of a Fireman and as time progressed become a 'Passed Fireman', enabling them to actually drive trains on occasions. It then became a case of 'waiting for dead men's shoes' before they eventually became a fully fledged driver. This could take upwards of twenty years. The vast majority of footplate crew took membership of **ASLEF** (Associated Society of Locomotive Enginemen and Firemen) a Union dating back to 1880. It was always **ASLEF** which wielded the greatest Union power on the railway and it remains so to this day. *GH1237*

Image 79: This is another beautifully atmospheric picture taken, once again, in the evening and from the same spot as the previous Image 78, but looking in the opposite direction. Here the 'Up' loop line signal has clearly fallen releasing the train and is it the driver or the fireman who throws up a salute to the signal man for giving it 'the road'; or is he waving to the cameraman? With the trees in full leaf and the shadows cast we can consider it a late summer or early autumn view. Being close to his home on the northern fringes of Bristol, George appears to have made a habit of making Westerleigh regular visits. This, perhaps, has to be the ultimate portrait of a very clean and well maintained 'Fowler Class 4' 43855 opening up as it pulls strongly away from the Yard with its 'Class D' freight. The fireman has prepared a good fire and there is steam to spare in the boiler. During its twilight years '43855' was shedded at Saltley (21A) for two years from November 1959 to December 1961, which looks commensurate with the period feel of this photograph. Having been built at Derby during the last year of the First World War and now over forty years old and looking sprightly it is still putting in good service on the main line with a Goods train bound for Washwood Heath or Water Orton Yards in Birmingham. A partially fitted 'Class D' was still considered to be an express freight but with only half of the vehicles fitted with the automatic brake. This would explain why the front half of the train consists entirely of four wheeled vans, all of which would have been so fitted with vacuum brake equipment. '43855' was last noted in the paint shop at Derby Works in June 1958 after undergoing a 'General Overhaul'. This may account for her well maintained appearance here; Saltley looked after it. It was eventually condemned in February 1963 after forty five years in service. *GH1249*

Image 80: Time has now moved on slightly but note how the railway infrastructure, buildings, embankments, permanent way etc. have yet to change from the standard to which the 1950's and previous generations was the norm. George has now climbed up to the gantry of the 'Up' loop line starter signal featured in the previous images. In this bird's eye view a Fowler designed 'Patriot Class' 4-6-0' 45519 'Lady Godiva' takes its leave from the Yard with an 'Up' freight. In 1958, due to their displacement from other sheds, where they had previously held sway on main line passenger duties, the 'Patriots' began to be dispatched elsewhere. As such in November 1958, this engine became re-allocated to Bristol (Barrow Road) (by then 82E) from West Coast main line duties at Carlisle Upperby (12B). At Barrow Road she quite possibly took on some of those duties previously carried out by the Fowler 'Goods' featured in the previous photograph. This train is possibly a 'Class 3/4' freight originating at Bristol (St. Philip's). If we look closely at the photograph only one footplate man (the driver) can be seen. My guess is that the fireman is crouched down with his head in the firebox door checking his fire. Just note all the infrastructure at the north end of Westerleigh Sidings. Not just the signal box but other structures such as the small cabin with its own fireplace which looks like a hut for a Foreman or wagon number taker perhaps. Then there's a small 'privy' for the signalman (and other staff), a sand box and oil barrel, for the use of footplate men, and a corrugated oil store for the signal lamp man. And who was Lady Godiva? She was an 11th century noblewoman, the wife of Leofric, the powerful Earl of Mercia and Lord of Coventry. As the story goes, Godiva was troubled by the crippling taxes Leofric had levied on the citizens of Coventry. After she repeatedly asked him to lessen the burden, Leofric said that he would only do so if she rode naked on horseback through the streets of Coventry. She called his bluff resulting in Leofric having to reduce the taxes. The legend was born and so the Midland Railway named this 'Patriot Class' engine after her. *GH1218*

Image 81: A view from the signal box looking north on a bright summer day as an unidentified 'Jubilee' Class engine coasts down the falling gradient approaching Westerleigh Sidings with its express. The engine is looking rather woebegone and bereft of nameplates. Although illegible the brevity of the carriage headboards could indicate this is a York-Bristol express. As was stated in Image 28 it is known that six 'Jubilees' were banished from Barrow Road shed at the end of August 1961 and dispatched to sheds further north. It heralded the end of the era for 'Jubilee' supremacy of express haulage on this route. The condition of the locomotive suggests this picture may then have been taken during that summer. The early evening shadows further suggest the train may be the 12.48pm ex York to Bristol, which according to a Working Timetable of the period was due at Mangotsfield, about five minutes further down the line, at 6.02pm. Note in the foreground the sleeper crossing, carrying a footpath across the railway at this very busy point, together with the obligatory 'Beware of Trains' and 'Trespass Warning' notices placed on each side of the tracks adjacent to the fence. Note too the Buffer Stop at the end of the head shunt, placed directly in front of the railway cottage window. I'm not sure I would be happy living there! The branch line curving away to the left is the northern end of the original Bristol and Gloucestershire Railway, built as a tramway in 1828 to carry coal from the mines in the Coalpit Heath area to the River Avon at Bristol. It became part of the Bristol and Gloucester Railway when the whole line was sold to the Midland Railway in 1845. It served a number of pits in the vicinity; latterly only three remained to pass into the ownership of the National Coal Board. Frog Lane and Mayshill Colliery were both closed by 1949. Nibley, the last remaining, continued to have rail access until 1953 and subsequently the branch was used for wagon storage as seen in this photograph. *GH1204*

Image 82: We have now arrived at Westerleigh village and from the road over bridge, which spans the railway at this point, we are looking north. From this point George captures 'Jubilee' 45642 'Boscawen' descending on the 1 in 286 falling gradient, towards Westerleigh North Junction, with its rake of eight ex-LMS Coaches. The entire train carries the early BR 'Blood and Custard' livery introduced in 1949 and the Brake Composite coach (BCK) behind the tender has an oval toilet window. This was the final development of this coach design which was referred to as 'porthole' stock. The building in the background marks the site of Dodmore Green Crossing and the Westerleigh North distant signal can just be seen to the right of it. As intimated earlier we are now in the heart of George's regular stamping ground, an easy bicycle ride from his home. Little appears to be known about 'Boscawen's' history and the shed code plate in the picture is illegible but she does look well turned out. It will be noted that fresh ballast has recently been dropped at regular intervals on the 'Up' line and is still awaiting packing. *GH0648*

Image 83: This picture looking at the bridge in the previous Image 82 was taken some years earlier, from just in front of the distance signal featured in that picture. On a lovely crisp morning a 'Fowler Class 4F' 44534 trundles north, its exhaust standing out under a clear blue sky, with its 'Class 9' 'pick-up' freight; most likely from Westerleigh Sidings to Barnwood, the LMR Sidings at Gloucester. If so it would be calling at the small intermediate stations along the way, picking up and dropping off wagons. Not too worried about the schedule and deep in thought the fireman is draped over the cab side with a fixed gaze. The cluster of buildings either side of the road over bridge form a large part of Westerleigh. For such a small village, never even warranting a 'Halt', it not only gave its name to the Sidings featured earlier but also, no less than five signal boxes. Westerleigh South and North boxes were situated one each end of the Sidings on the Midland main line. Westerleigh East and Westerleigh West Junctions sat on the Great Western main line, linking the base of the Westerleigh triangle, whilst Westerleigh North Junction was at the apex of the triangle towards Yate. This is not to mention Westerleigh Viaduct where the Great Western main line spanned the Midland mainline. Such were the intricacies of Victorian and Edwardian built railways. Not unsurprisingly the locomotive featured in this photograph was based at Barrow Road (22A) for thirteen years from June 1950 to June 1963. In May 1958 it was noted in the Erecting Shop at Derby Works undergoing an Intermediate Overhaul. It had entered service from Crewe Works in September 1928, so by the time this picture was taken was probably around thirty years old. Towards the end of the mass culling of these locomotives it was withdrawn from Barrow Road in November 1964; by then probably one of the last of its breed. *GH1227*

Image 84: A little further north we witness the unseemly sight of a 'Jubilee' reduced to working a lowly 'Class 7' 'unfitted express freight'. Showing a clean exhaust she is still accelerating away, heading north, from Westerleigh Yard. The train is just passing the 'Down' Westerleigh North distant signal on the opposite side of the tracks, referred to in the previous images, with a rake of BR metal mineral wagons. Her outward appearance suggests this as an early 1960's photograph. With the splasher, carrying her nameplate, obscured by steam it cannot be seen whether or not '45598' 'Basutoland' is still carrying a nameplate. But she does have one of those hallmarks of a latter day LMR steam engine; a yellow diagonal stripe on the side of her cab. This denoted that for safety reasons the locomotive was not allowed to work under the overhead electric wires on the London Midland Region. But it also acted as a visual reminder to footplate men, as they climbed aboard the locomotive, not to climb onto the tender to bring forward coal. It was originally introduced when the Euston to Crewe electrification went live in 1960 but seems to have been subsequently extended as the electrification of the West Coast main line progressed. According to records it was probably as a result of this transition that, in July 1961, seventeen 'Jubilees' were transferred to Burton (17B), displacing Fowler Class 4F' engines. 'Basutoland' was one of these, moving from Derby (17A) where she had been resident for the previous two years. The shed code plate displayed here could be either. *GH0732*

Image 85: We are still very much in the same position as the previous two images 83 & 84, but now farther back in time and on a summer morning. Indeed this may be one of George's earlier photographs. Here we see 'Jubilee' 45663 'Jervis' looking in presentable condition and with a clean trail of exhaust evaporating into a hazy sky, easing its way along the level approaching Dodmore Green Crossing at Westerleigh. The view of the train from rail level adds impact to the picture. This has to be an early to mid-1950's decade northbound express with a rake of ex-LMS coaches. One can actually imagine George basking in the sunshine on the trackside awaiting the train's approach; such was the tranquillity of the age. 'Jervis' was a long-time Barrow Road (22A) engine until the tide turned for the Jubilees in the early 1960's. In January 1958 she had been transferred from Bristol to Derby and whilst still operating on this route a further move, eighteen months later, took her off to Patricroft (26F) in Manchester and she stayed in the north-west until being withdrawn in October 1964, after almost thirty years service. Notice the slim signal post on the 'Down' side with its signal arm shrouded in steam. As stated in the previous image, this steel post carried the Westerleigh North distant signal. However, unlike that picture the post here is painted in black and white. According to Warburton in his book 'A Pictorial Record of LMS Signals' it was a policy applied to isolated distant signals. The reason is not known. It was also LMS policy to repaint steel signal posts every five years but the practice was discontinued just prior to nationalisation. Many such posts remained unpainted well into the 1950's as in this instance. GH0071

Image 86: This is a lovely picture, taken in fading evening light and has to have been taken in late summer. The long grasses are yellowing and smoke is drifting from the chimneys of a couple of houses in Westerleigh village. Storming towards Dodmore Green crossing is 'Black Five' 45274 at the head of its train of 'perishables; a complete rake of four wheeled ventilated vans, more fruit and vegetables for the Midland and Northern markets. The locomotive's shed plate code cannot be discerned but '45274' was working this route for eight years from nationalisation day (01/01/48) through to the end of 1956. It had stints at Saltley (21A), Bournville (21B), then back to Saltley, on to Barrow Road (22A) and Leeds (Holbeck) (20A) before being moved off to Cricklewood (14A). So it can confidently be said the picture dates to the first half of the 1950's. Dodmore Green crossing in the foreground was quite a substantial well maintained sleeper crossing, shown on the One Inch to the Mile Ordnance Survey map of the area as a 'Road used as a public path'. It can be seen that the crossing is entirely uncontrolled with the statutory sign and notice displayed. On the eastern side a fenced track led up to it but on the western side this petered out to a simple bridleway and farmland. Private crossings such as this were installed by the railway when it was built, for the benefit of farmers and others whose land or access to dwellings was divided by the railway. They were also known as 'accommodation' or 'occupation' crossings, many still exist. Dodmore Green was just such a crossing. *GH0094*

Image 87: This occupation crossing was probably unique in that it had a house built on the grand scale sitting next to it, hard by the railway. What could be the explanation for such a building? With its close proximity to the tracks it has to have been a railway connected house; quite possibly for a crossing keeper. The old Bristol and Gloucestershire Railway, a horse drawn mineral line connecting pits in the Coalpit Heath area to Bristol, opened in stages between 1832 and 1834. A decade later the Bristol & Gloucester Railway, originally being built by the GWR, was acquired by the Midland Railway in 1845. The B&G's line absorbed the former mineral line joining it about a mile south of Dodmore at Westerleigh, probably traversing the same landed estate as that including the line at Dodmore Crossing. During the Victorian era it was often the case for the landowner, when selling land upon which a railway was to be built, to insert conditions with which the railway company had to comply, e.g. provision of a private station, a tunnel, the use of certain architecture or a requirement for certain buildings such as a crossing keepers house. The landowner here, requiring the construction of a crossing keepers house, would previously have been used only to trains hauled by horsepower. Whoever required it could never have imagined that one day noisy, heavy and fast moving steam trains would be thundering past it at very close quarters. This theory, of course, is pure conjecture but what else might be the reason? Its origins may well remain a mystery. In bright early morning sunshine George recorded Stanier 'Jubilee' 45685 'Barfleur', traversing the crossing with an 'Up' express from Temple Meads. The earliest of these was probably the 8.40am to the north-east. 'Barfleur' was based at Barrow Road (22A) right through from nationalisation day at the beginning of 1948 until April 1964 when she was withdrawn. *GH1851*

Image 88: Turning the camera around we now have another 1950's view, this time of a 'Down' express approaching the crossing. The same house occupies the left hand side of the picture with Westerleigh Viaduct in the background. An immaculate 'Jubilee' 45572 'Eire' boasting a Barrow Road (22A) shed plate breezes effortlessly along heading home. She was one of the long-standing 'Jubilees' posted to Barrow Road from at least 1948 through to August 1961 when she became one of the six, surplus to requirements and dispatched north. But here she is still in her heyday. Without any distinct shadows on a bright day suggests the sun is in the south and high in the sky, therefore it would be around lunch time, so she may be heading home with the 7.32am ex-Bradford due through Mangotsfield at 1.13pm and at Temple Meads at 1.24pm. Its rake of ten coaches are pure ex-LMS, ninety per cent of them 'Staniers'. In 1932, William Stanier took up his appointment as Chief Mechanical Engineer to the LMS and one of his first tasks was to modernise the coaching fleet. His first, of the completely flush sided coaches, emerged soon after. This design continued to be built for several years after 1947 until the introduction of the BR Mark 1 design in 1951. The second coach behind the tender is of much earlier design, probably dating back to the LMS Period 1 stock of the 1920's. *GH1413*

Image 89: We are in exactly the same position for this photograph but this time in the evening with the crossing house now casting long shadows across the track. Whether he knew of this movement or he just heard it trundling towards him, George nevertheless, could not resist the opportunity to record it, whatever it was. It looks like one of the first generation two axle tamping machines. Hitherto all track maintenance had been carried out manually and was very labour intensive. In 1953 the first hydraulic operated track tamping machine was put into use. It marked a new approach, introducing technology. The two-axle machine had a 3.5 metre wheelbase and an overall length of 9 metres. Its tamping units were located between the axles and the levelling and lifting of the track was still undertaken manually. They came to be known as 'Plassers', the name of their developer, and this would appear to be one of those machines. The unit is carrying the equivalent of a 'Class J' headlamp code indicating a 'Through mineral or empty wagon train'; a single lamp to the left of the buffer beam which of course this unit does not have. Presumably this code was also applied to these units when they were first introduced. It also has the correct tail lamp at the rear. The alphabetic headlamp coding was changed in 1962 to accommodate the introduction of national four character train reporting numbers. This machine has a crew of five; four sitting wherever they could find space and one hidden away in the cab driving it. It looks a very 'Heath-Robinson' affair but was the forerunner of the modern equipment in use today. *GH1411*

Image 90: We are still on the 'Up' side, i.e. the western side of the line, now midway between Dodmore Green Crossing and Westerleigh Viaduct. But time has moved on significantly as George records a 'BR Class 9F' 2-10-0 92118 powering north with a 'Class 3/4' train of perishables, again comprised of four wheeled ventilated vans. The driver looks out as if aware of the likelihood of George's presence. From what can be counted there are at least thirty vehicles in the consist and probably more. It has to be remembered that sixty years ago the country was much more reliant on home grown, rather than imported, food and most of it was transported by rail. Because the traffic was seasonal the railway authorities had to be nimble with their planning. Many of these trains would not appear in the standard Working Timetable but added in Weekly Notices as requirements dictated. Therefore the trains would not necessarily be carrying reporting numbers. The 9F's were the absolute final development of steam engines on British Railways and regrettably always living on borrowed time. '92118' was released into service from Crewe Works at the very end of 1956. From January 1962 it was allocated to Saltley (21A), which shed code it is carrying here, until July 1964. This gives a two and a half years window during which this picture could have been taken. It was finally withdrawn from Carnforth (10A) in May 1968; at the death of steam. It only had a service life of barely eleven and a half years. Note in the background a full view of the building seen in previous images at Dodmore Green Crossing. *GH0374*

Image 91: The tranquil calm of Westerleigh is broken as Fowler 'Patriot' Class 45519 'Lady Godiva' steams north with its evening express. The fields have been mown, the hay gathered into piles ready for the binder and the shadows are lengthening. George has captured the atmosphere of a late summer evening perfectly. The contrast of the picture is also right, just look at the shadow cast by the train across the far field. The clock in the church tower of St. James the Great in Westerleigh Village must be getting ready to strike eight o'clock. 'Lady Godiva' had been allocated to Barrow Road (82E) in November 1958 and is seen here probably during the following year. In the summer Working Timetable 1959, the York and Newcastle passenger and postal train left Temple Meads at 7.25pm followed on Fridays only by the 7.45pm to York, seemingly running as a relief passenger train. This could have been either. More likely the latter; both were timed to pass Yate twenty three minutes after departing Temple Meads which meant the postal, after a call at Mangotsfield, passing Westerleigh at about 7.44pm and the relief at about 8.2pm. '45519's' heritage can be traced back to 1920. In 1912 Charles John Bowen-Cooke CME of the LNWR introduced the 'Claughton' Class of express engines. Subsequently in 1930 Henry Fowler designed the 'Patriot' Class totalling 52 engines. The first two engines of the Class were rebuilds of 'Claughton' locomotives, retaining their wheels and other details. Fowler then built a further 50 in the same manner. In the case of 'Lady Godiva' this was ex-LNWR No.110 (LMS No. 6008) which had been released from Crewe Works in September 1920 and had her name bestowed upon her in May 1923. She was withdrawn in December 1932. Her parts were used in the construction of this 'Lady Godiva' which was released from Crewe in February 1933. *GH1390*

Image 92: A very forlorn looking ex-GWR '4300 Class' 2-6-0 7320 emerges from beneath the south side of Westerleigh Viaduct at the head of a four coach stopping train. The ex-Midland shed at Gloucester (Barnwood), by then (85C), had closed on the 4th May 1964 and thereafter motive power for the Gloucester to Temple Meads stopping services was provided by the former Western shed at Gloucester (Horton Road) (85B). After working much of its later life in South Wales during its twilight years, '7320' had been transferred from there to Taunton, by then (83B), in August 1964 but was only there for barely a month before being sent on to Horton Road. It was withdrawn from service in early November. This then suggests the picture would have been taken during the early autumn of 1964. During that period the shadows indicate the most likely train this could be is the 4.5pm from Gloucester (Eastgate) to Temple Meads, which would be due to pass this point around 5.10pm. The whole stopping service only lasted to January 1965 when it was also withdrawn. The Great Western '4300' Mogul class, first introduced by Churchward in 1911 was considered to be the company's 'maid of all work', clearly a tribute to the reliability of these engines which carried right through to their demise. '7320' entered service from Swindon Works in April 1925 and at the time of its withdrawal had been in service for approaching forty years. *GH1370*

Image 93: We have now arrived at Westerleigh Viaduct or to be precise beneath it. A fine atmospheric action shot records a 'Black Five' powering beneath the viaduct with a 'Class 6', 'express freight with not less than a fifth of the train's vehicles fitted with the vacuum brake'. The headlamp code for this is one lamp on the centre of the buffer beam and one over the right buffer, as seen from the front. The telegraph wires here, in front of the train, were on the 'Down' side therefore the train is heading north. The sun fairly low in the sky behind the train and the billowing exhaust suggests an autumn morning. It is an essay in light and shade. George would have been up early because the only real contender for this train would be the 'Class 6' 7.25 am Westerleigh Sidings to Toton. Toton is between Derby and Nottingham and during the period of the photograph was the location of a vast marshalling yard. The only decipherable numbers on the locomotive are '4469X' however research of the relevant numbering sequence reveals only two possibilities. '44690' was based at Derby (17A) during the winter of 1958/59 and from 1963 to 1966. '44691' was based at the same depot for short periods from June 1958 to February 1959 and again from October 1960 to June 1961. *GH1374*

Image 94: It is a beautiful English late summer day; the grasses are beginning to turn golden. A polished 'Black Five, 44805 emerges from beneath Westerleigh Viaduct forging north with its four coach 'Up' stopping train. With the shadows being cast beneath the viaduct the sun appears to be moving into the western sky giving the idea this is probably a late afternoon or early evening photograph. Released new from Derby Works in June 1944 '44805' likely went straight to Saltley (21A); it was certainly there at nationalisation on 1st January 1948. In this picture it still has 'Saltley' emblazoned on its front buffer beam indicating an early decade photograph, but it remained allocated there until 1965. A WTT of the period shows two contenders as to which train this may be. The first would be the 5.15pm stopping train from Temple Meads to Birmingham New Street due at Yate at 5.48pm. The other, and possibly more likely, would be the 6.30pm from BTM expected to arrive at Yate at 7.1pm. Some train travel in former years could be very tiresome! *GH1382*

Image 95: Viewed from the east just south of Westerleigh Viaduct over a wild flower strewn meadow, across which giant electricity pylons stride, we now see a Fowler 'Class 4F' 0-6-0 heading south with a train which has to be some kind of van train. Regrettably the identity of the locomotive cannot be established but is likely to be a Barrow Road (22A) or Gloucester Barnwood based locomotive. Alternatively it may even have come from farther afield at Saltley (21A). After the 'Grouping' of the railways in 1923, Barnwood was allocated the coding (M7). From February 1935 the LMS re-coded the shed as (22B), a coding it carried through to a re-organisation of regional boundaries by BR, from the beginning of February 1958, when it was re-coded as (85E). Throughout the 1950's there was always more than a large handful of Fowler 4F's shedded at both Barnwood and Barrow Road providing the mainstay of power for freight traffic between the two cities. The van train in this picture is a complete miscellany of vehicles. The leading coach behind the tender is what appears to be a Period 1 LMS coach dating back to the 1920's and designed by Sir Henry Fowler hence these being referred to as 'Fowler' coaches. Then comes a four wheeled ventilated van followed by an aged bogie full brake van, two more four wheeled vans and finally a much more modern ex-LMS bogie brake van in crimson lake and cream livery. As for what train it was likely to be we shall never know but with a consist of this form, all the vehicles would likely be fitted with the vacuum brake. *GH1353*

Image 96: On a hazy summer day there is a stranger on the tracks; an unrebuilt 'Battle of Britain' Pacific' 34079 '141 Squadron' glides north beneath Westerleigh Viaduct, with a heavy through train from the Southern Region to the north. '34079' was allocated to Exmouth Junction (72A) from February 1958 to September 1964, previously having been employed on the South-Eastern Section of the Southern Region. So what was she doing here on Midland Region metals? She would have arrived at Bath Green Park (82F) over the Somerset and Dorset line, possibly having worked through with a train from one or more of the East Devon seaside resorts. At Green Park the engine would have required to be serviced and turned. But it would not be unusual, during a busy summer period, for such an engine available on shed to be used on a filling in turn; in this case perhaps taking another train as far as Gloucester. The leading vehicles look like BR Mark 1 coaches introduced during the early 1950's and there is even the possibility of a Restaurant Car in the middle of the train. The indication of the locomotive's allocation suggests this photograph would have been taken in the late 1950's or very early 1960's. Note how the express train headlamp code is replicated by the two Southern Region Disc Codes above the lamps. *GH0514*

Image 97: The motive power seen at this location during the early 1960's became quite varied. In this view an ex-GWR 'Grange Class' 4-6-0 6814 'Enborne Grange' effortlessly gallops north with an eleven coach express. Without displaying a 'TRN' gives the impression this would be a regular service. That impression is spoiled by the inclusion in the make-up of a non-corridor compartment coach immediately behind the tender. 'Enborne Grange' was based at Bristol (St. Philips Marsh) (82B) from June 1962 until her withdrawal in December 1963, which gives a time frame as to when the picture may have been taken. As will be seen later (see Image 138) many ex-GWR locomotives experienced a premature demise because of the unavailability of spare parts, due to their 'non-standard' design. Alas, as a result, 'Enborne Grange's' demise was premature. In this picture there isn't any hint of escaping steam and the locomotive appears to be in total command of its train. Under the management of Charles Collett the 'Granges' became the replacements for the ageing '4300' Class' and were designated as the GWR equivalent of any 'Class 5' mixed traffic locomotive (i.e. 'Black Fives'), although on the Western their principal employment was on freight traffic; hence her allocation to St. Philips Marsh, essentially a freight shed. Such locomotives were regularly pressed into passenger train duties during busy periods in the summer which probably accounts for her appearance here. *GH1380*

Image 98: Another fine summer evening picture; which sees a very young Richard Heiron sitting up in his period pram, parked in the middle of cornfield stubble to watch the trains go by. In this case Richard was having quite a late evening. Here George records another 'Black Five' 44989 trundling north with a 'Class 5' freight (An express freight with the automatic brake operative on not fewer than half of the vehicles), as in this case exemplified by all the vans formed up next to the locomotive. '44989' was based at Burton (17B) from May 1963 to July 1965 which gives an indication of the period during which the photograph was taken. In a WTT of the time the only train that appears to be the contender was the 7.00pm (FSX) Bristol (St. Philip's) to Derby (St. Mary's) which was due to leave Westerleigh Sidings, after a call, at 7.55pm. It then ran to Gloucester (Eastgate), stopping there for water, Barnwood Sidings, probably for a crew change and then at Bromsgrove, again to take on more water and no doubt pick up banking assistance for the climb of the Lickey Incline. I expect Richard fell asleep on his way home after the excitement of watching this train roll by. *GH1359*

Image 99: This is an absolutely lovely scene; taken towards the setting sun on a springtime evening, as shown by the blossom on the bush in the foreground. We are now at Rodford less than a mile further on where George obviously saw this old gnarled tree and used it as both a frame and his point of perspective to capture this very artistic and arresting view. One of the ubiquitous ex-Midland Fowler 'Class '4F" 0-4-0's, which looks suspiciously like '43953', heads a very mixed assortment of vans and wagons past Yate South Junction 'Up' Distant Signal. Throughout a decade from June 1949 to April 1959 this engine was consistently noted on its home shed displaying a Bristol Barrow Road (22A) shed code plate. With the change of regional boundaries it became 82E and the engine's shed code plate was changed accordingly. By the Carriers Act of 1830 the railways were considered to be Common Carriers. But the Railway and Canal Traffic Act 1854 placed additional obligations on the railways due to their monopoly status. Each railway company was now required to take all trade offered and to set and publish the same levels of fares to all, in respect of any particular service. This situation continued with the nationalisation of the railways in 1948. By the end of 1960 BR had accumulated a deficit of £500 million. The Transport Act 1962 remedied this, but ironically also enacted the recommendations of the Beeching Report which led to the closure of so much of the railway infrastructure. *GH0108*

Image 100: We are still at exactly the same location, as in the previous image but George has now turned his camera to the south taking another opportunity to use his artistic eye. He had discovered this tree beside a lane running almost parallel with the railway. He used it again to frame this picture of an unidentified 'Jubilee Class' engine running north with an express, made up of a mix of nine, mainly ex LMS, coaches. This indicates a photograph from the early half of the decade. An interesting feature of this picture is the railway architecture and furniture. Note the platelayer's hut on the extreme left, next to the farm track under-bridge leading into the fields beyond. It appears to be built quite substantially in brick at the base of the embankment. Then on the far side of the tracks in front of the locomotive we can see a milepost which is in the right position to mark 121 miles from Derby via Whitacre. The reason for this is a throwback to Midland Railway days when mileages were measured by the shortest route to St. Pancras, here being approximately 210 miles away via Derby, hence extraordinarily making the northbound, an 'Up' line. The Midland subsequently revised this to make London Road Junction at Derby the new starting point for this route. On the nearside of the line is a gradient post and this is roughly where a level section of track began to rise at a grade of 1 in 393 for a short section before Yate South Junction. For the entire decade and just beyond; until they were superseded by the emerging 'Peak Class' diesels, the 'Jubilees' held sway as the predominant express locomotives on this route.
GH0607

Left Image 101: A well presented BR 'Class 9F' 2-10-0 92150 coasts south, on the 'Down' Midland main line, past the 'Up' side Yate South Junction distant signal. It is in charge of a 'Class 8' ('through freight not fitted with the automatic brake'). Behind the telegraph pole, to the right, the outline of the 'Up' Westerleigh loop line can be seen. On delivery from Crewe Works on 31st October 1957 '92150' was delivered to Westhouses (18B), a shed in the coal mining area of North Derbyshire. After serving there for just over a year it was reallocated to Saltley (21A), the code displayed on its smoke box door in this photograph. During October 1961 '92150' was noted by a Stephenson Locomotive Society correspondent in the Erecting Shop at Crewe Works, no doubt in the middle of an overhaul. This may explain the engine's condition in this photograph. In a Working Timetable of the period the weekday 1.30pm 'Class 8' Washwood Heath to Westerleigh Yard would be passing this point just after seven o'clock in the evening, a time commensurate with the shadows thrown in the picture. This would be a slow train conveying general merchandise. The first vehicle behind the tender appears to be an ex-LMS design four wheeled Covered Carriage Truck. The second is a BR Mark 1 CCT, a type of railway van with end doors used for moving motor cars or parcel traffic. On a train of this sort they would both probably be conveying miscellaneous goods. The third vehicle is a bogie bolster wagon designed to carry long thin cargoes such as timber or rails and other steel sections. The remainder of the train visible comprises BR mineral wagons. *GH0814*

Above Image 102: Marginally further north George has taken up a position on the bridge which carried a lane from Rodford to Nibley over the Midland main line. The Yate South Junction distant signal can just be made out in the jaws of the bridge of the old Coalpit Heath mineral railway, which burrowed its way beneath the ex-GWR South Wales main line in the background. Into this scene we now see the 'Up' 'Cornishman' beginning the short climb up to Yate South Junction. It is headed by an unidentified Frederick Hawksworth designed 'County Class' locomotive. As we have seen earlier this Western Region train ran via the ex-Midland route between Bristol and Yate rather than the Western route. It is carrying the pre-1960 'TRN 675' the designated number for the 'Up' working which left Penzance at 10.30am. Separately, the South Devon portion of the train left Kingswear at 12.15pm and stopped at most stations till it reached Exeter. It called at Newton Abbot and usually carried the headboard but it was, then, not an 'A' class train; it was a semi-fast with many stops, and just four carriages. It was hauled by a Newton Abbot engine that had gone down to Kingswear and turned there earlier. At Exeter, the Devon portion combined with the Cornwall portion and went forward, behind the Laira (83D engine) to Bristol, due there about 4 pm. Here it would be replaced by a Wolverhampton (Stafford Road) (84A) engine which would take the train through to Wolverhampton, due there at 7.25pm. Taking account of the ex-GWR coaching stock on this train this locomotive can probably be whittled down to one of three; '1018 County of Leicester', 1019 County of Merioneth' or '1029 County of Worcester', each of which was allocated to Stafford Road between January 1953 and October 1954 potentially making this a summer photograph of that period. *GH1432*

Opposite Top Image 103: This picture is taken from exactly the same position as the previous Image 102 but this time looking north at the steel girder bridge which carried the 'Up' Westerleigh loop line over the Midland main line. Drifting beneath this bridge is a very trim looking Caprotti fitted 'Black Five' 44743 with steam almost shut off and valves faintly feathering, drifting effortlessly along on the favourable gradient. '44743' was delivered new from Crewe Works on 26th June 1948 and Barrow Road (22A) was probably its first allocation. The engine was then re-allocated to Derby (17A) in April/May 1957 before spending the rest of its service in the north-west. It's heading a 'Down' express for Bristol composed principally of pre-nationalisation coaches with, possibly, some BR Mark 1's towards the rear of the train which gives the picture a mid-decade feel. The first coach behind the tender appears to be an ex GWR coach, probably built during the late 1920's. Following are two ex-LMS Period 3, Stanier designed flush sided coaches from the mid 1930's, so this cross country express is made up of a mixture of coaching stock which one might expect to have seen during early BR days. GH1434

Opposite Bottom Image 104: The original Bristol and Gloucester main line and both Westerleigh curves came together at Yate South Junction. It is at this location that an unidentified 'Hall', emitting smoke from a very dirty fire, emerges off the loop onto the main line heading north with 'TRN H37'. In the 1960 summer timetable this number was assigned to the 11.10am (SO) Penzance-Wolverhampton (Low Level). The locomotive, not looking in the best of conditions, is hauling thirteen coaches. With only a mixed traffic locomotive in command this might be expected to present time-keeping problems. On close inspection of the photograph the engine's shed code plate looks suspiciously like 84B. At this time Oxley (84B) still had a healthy supply of 'Halls' to supplement the dwindling numbers of passenger engines at Stafford Road (84A). Running forty minutes behind the northbound 'Cornishman' this train probably acted as some form of 'sweeper-up'; carrying passengers, who for one reason or another, were unable to board the 'Cornishman' along the way. During the 1950's Yate South Junction signal box would have been very busy handling trains converging from the two routes onto one to carry them north to Standish Junction before the tracks divided once again. GH0803

Below Image 105: At the same location, but from the opposite side of the tracks, George caught the 'Up' 'Devonian' also coming off the same curve from Westerleigh at Yate South Junction. On this occasion he takes this back-lit photograph into the watery sunlight which reflects off the boiler off 'Jubilee' 45662 'Kempenfelt', an engine which spent most of its life based at Barrow Road (22A). With the first vehicle behind the tender being a BR Mark 1 Brake Composite (BCK) we may assume this is a second half of the decade picture. Meanwhile on the ex-Midland line from Mangotsfield one of the ubiquitous Fowler 'Class 4F' engines is being held at the junction 'Up' home signal in order to allow its passage. In a Freight Train WTT of the same period there was an 11.20am Bristol (St. Philip's) to Washwood Heath 'Class 8' (Through freight train not fitted with the automatic brake); i.e. a slow goods train made up of a mixed assortment of trucks, vans and other wagons. If that was the goods train in this picture it would have been due to leave Westerleigh Sidings at 12.55pm which would mean either it was running early or the 'Devonian' was running slightly late. The most unusual feature is that the 'Fowler' is running tender first over such a long distance and there is no indication in the timetable that there was any change of engine en-route, but if there was this would have probably occurred at Barnwood. GH2207

Image 106: Taken from the A432 road bridge just north of Yate station George had a rare opportunity to photograph an ex-LNER Thompson designed 'Class B1' 61051 coasting through on the falling gradient of 1 in 453 with a northbound summer express running under 'TRN 1E68'. Introduction of a totally revised system of Reporting Numbers became effective from 13th June 1960 when Train Identification Headlamp Codes were changed from letters to numerals. The new system used a 4 digit code. The first represented the class of train, 1 being express, the second digit represented the region to which the train was destined, and were 'all Regions wide' to cover for those trains that began on one region and ended on another. So depending on the actual day the photograph was taken this train could be either the 9.5am (M-FO) Paignton to Sheffield or the 12.4pm (QSO) Weston-super-Mare to Sheffield. The letter 'Q' in the WTT indicated the train ran as required. It is interesting to note that until the mid 1960's, am/pm times continued to be shown in railway timetables. Western Region were the first to officially adopt the 24 hour clock for the summer timetable introduced on 15th June 1964. Other regions subsequently followed suit. '61051' was allocated to Sheffield Darnall (41A) from June 1956 to June 1963, so there is little doubt as to where the train is destined. But look at the attention to detail still being displayed by country stations in 1961. The neatness of Yate station is self evident; the bed of plants on the upside platform, surrounded by white painted boulders is planted in regimental rows; evidently it is still early summer. Note also in the background the buildings of a thriving Agricultural Construction Company, testimony to the rural surroundings of Yate. *GH0673*

Image 107: George Heiron became renowned for his night-time photography which peaked with his well known images taken at Badminton sometimes on snow covered winter evenings. But as well as Temple Meads and Mangotsfield another of those locations where he honed these skills was Yate. Note how he had set up his lighting from the right. It is here, on an autumn/winter evening he took this photograph of 'Jubilee Class' 45668 'Madden' waiting at Yate at the head of what is most likely to be the 6.30pm semi-fast from Temple Meads to Birmingham (New Street) which was due to stand at Yate from 6.59pm to 7.1pm giving George the opportunity to set up his time-delay photograph to ensure a crisp picture. It has to be agreed that the result is superb; all aspects of the photograph are exposed to perfection. This laggardly train ran via Worcester (Shrub Hill) where it stood from 9.1pm to 9.19pm, while mails were likely to have been sorted. It took almost four hours to complete the journey to New Street where it was due at 10.26pm. 'Madden' was based at Derby (17A) from October 1959 before moving on to Burton (17B) in November 1961, which gives us a timeframe for when this picture may have been taken.' Madden' was another of the 'Jubilees' named after distinguished Naval Officers. Admiral of the Fleet Sir Charles Edward Madden, was a Royal Navy officer who served during WWI as Chief of the Staff to Jellicoe in the Grand Fleet from 1914 to 1916 and as Second-in-Command of the fleet under Sir David Beatty from 1916 to 1919. Another point of interest is the small wagon turntable to the right of the picture in front of the Goods Shed. At the time the previous image 106 was taken some of the lines leading to it had been removed. *GH0808*

Image 108: George obviously continued to visit Yate during evenings into the diesel area to continue working on his night-time photography. This picture records a **BR Type 4 'Peak Class' Diesel Electric D29** during a call at Yate. This is another success with the picture clearly showing the cab lit up with the driver and secondman awaiting the 'right away'. The 'Peaks' were in the vanguard of the earliest mainline diesels produced. The first ten, gained the sobriquet, due to each being given the name of an English or Welsh mountain peak. They produced 2,300 horsepower. Subsequent members of the Class, of which 'D29' was one, were produced with a greater horsepower of 2,500. There were one hundred and ninety-three locomotives of the combined Classes built. 'D29' was delivered new from Derby Works (17A) on 13th May 1961 but was very soon re-allocated to Leeds, first at Neville Hill (55H) from June 1961 and then Holbeck (55A) until August 1968. The 6.30pm semi-fast Temple Meads to Birmingham (New Street) still ran in the Winter 1960/61 Western Region public timetable, valid until 11th June 1961 but there was also a later stopping train from Temple Meads to Gloucester (Eastgate) which called at Yate at 10.15pm, which could be the train in this picture. *GH0811*

Image 109: The platforms are deserted as a southbound freight scurries through Yate. From the shadows cast and the 'Up' platform flower bed being in the same condition as in the previous Image 108 there is some evidence to suggest the two pictures were taken on the same evening. The first two trucks are loaded with pulverised coal and therefore likely to be unfitted with vacuum brake equipment. Looking closely at the picture it can be seen that the right hand home signal on the bracket beyond the station has been cleared for the main line on to Westerleigh. Those two facts would tend to suggest this would be another 'Class 8' freight, the most likely contender being our old friend from Image 101, the 1.30pm Washwood Heath to Westerleigh Yard which would be passing Yate at about 7:00pm, but such trains would often be running late. In charge of this train is a fairly clean looking Stanier 'Class 8F' 48220 in full steam as it approaches the last few hundred yards climb at 1 in 453 towards Yate South Junction. It was based at Saltley (21A) form January 1959 to September 1962. After a brief spell re-allocated to Annesley (16D) in Nottinghamshire it was then returned to Saltley in December of the same year, serving there once more until November 1964 when it was moved on to Oxley (2B). This picture could have been taken during either period. *GH0807*

Image 110: It must be a Saturday and the 'Rovers' must be playing at home. A group of men sit on a bench seat beside the 'gentlemen's urinal' on the 'Down' platform at Yate. They appear to be in deep discussion, possibly about the game they may be heading to watch. Are they a contingent of fans of Bristol Rovers football club, who at that time played their home matches at Eastville stadium, an easy walking distance from Fishponds station? Into this scene comes another 'BR' Standard Class 5', this time '73003' at the head of a stopping train made up of two bogie parcel vans and four coaches. '73003' was allocated to Barrow Road (22A) from January 1958 until March 1963, which gives us a good timeframe for the period of the photograph. With that information and were the scenario to be true then this train could well have been the 12.00 noon Gloucester Eastgate to Temple Meads. It was due at Yate at 12.57pm and to arrive at Fishponds at 1.11pm giving ample time for 'a pint' and to then make their way to the ground ready for a three o'clock kick-off. If they were not going for a drink then it would be the 1.18pm from Gloucester due Yate at 2.16pm and Fishponds at 2.33pm. There is much evidence in this picture of the station's origins. The buildings on both platforms are very much of a Brunelian design reflecting back to their origin on the Bristol and Gloucester Railway. Opened in 1844 and built to the 7ft. Broad Gauge, it was acquired by the Midland Railway in 1845 and converted to Standard Gauge. As with most rural stations of the period Yate appears to be kept in very good order; note, too, the two types of porter's barrow waiting in readiness for use on the 'Up'-side platform. *GH0812*

Image 111: According to the shadows across the platform it is late afternoon or early evening as an 'Up' stopping train disgorges its passengers at Yate. Is that scarf, worn by the first gentleman, in football club colours or are the men returning home from Bristol on a commuter service? From the evidence of the picture with two of the men looking back to another disappearing back onto the train someone has left something behind. The safety valve is blowing furiously on the unidentified 'Black Five' at the front of the train even though it had passed the summit at Yate South and the next stretch of the journey is all downhill to Wickwar and Charfield. One of the footplate crew looks back waiting for the green flag from the Guard. The neat borders at the back of the platform have been cleared of their summer growth and the trees in the background beyond the bridge have lost their leaves so it is probably autumn, namely the football season. Running every day during the period of the photograph, the 5.15pm from Temple Meads called at Fishponds at 5.26pm (where it would probably collect football supporters if it was a Saturday) and was due at Yate at 5.47pm or it could otherwise have been the 6.30pm from Temple Meads due Yate at 7pm. The signal box visible beneath the bridge is Yate Main Line Junction and the home signal on the left side of the bracket is for the Thornbury Branch. *GH0809*

Image 112: Back on the A432,(see Image 106) but now looking north, George photographed a 'BR Standard Class 5' 73047 passing Yate Main Line Junction signal box with a short express consisting of only five coaches. Three of them are BR Mark 1 coaches, the other two appear to be former LMS designs. '73047' went new from Derby Works on 8th December 1953 to Sheffield Millhouses (19B) and was allocated there until July/August 1955 when it was sent to Bath (Green Park) (71G). Given its time worn appearance; the question therefore may be; which train is this? During the late 1950's a number of trains ran from the north-eastern area direct to Bournemouth on summer Saturdays. As an example, in the 1959 WTT, one of these was the 09.35am Sheffield to Bournemouth West due past Yate at 1.51pm, but during that period there were a number of others following, one right after the other. There is much of interest in this photograph. Opposite the signal box and curving away to the left is the former Thornbury branch. The Yate to Thornbury branch had closed to passenger traffic by 19th June 1944 but remained in use serving a quarry at Tytherington until, in 2013, the quarry was mothballed. However on 19th November 2021 the line was reopened to serve Tytherington Quarry once again. The owners, Hanson, planned to operate trains from Tytherington to Appleford, Oxfordshire. Trains were expected to comprise of up to 42 wagons. In the Goods Yard to the right a BR Scammell Scarab road vehicle can be glimpsed. Between 1948 and 1967 these vehicles were widely used across the system for deliveries from Goods Yards to the local area. *GH0801*

Image 113: About a mile north of Yate a BR Standard Class 9F 2-10-0 92248 puts on steam as it begins the gentle southbound climb of 1 in 312 heading towards Yate near 'milepost 119'. Its headlamp code tells us it is an unfitted through freight train, that appears largely comprised of loaded coal wagons. This is quite a late Heiron steam photograph. '92248' was not released from Crewe Works until 2nd December 1958. It started life at Ebbw Junction (Newport) (86A) before moving to Saltley (21A) for a year, in September 1959 until September 1960, when it was re-allocated to Barrow Road (82E) until February 1965. It is not possible to read the shed code plate the engine is carrying, but its dishevelled appearance suggests the photograph was likely to have been taken during its time at Barrow Road. This was a time when 'Train Reporting Numbers', required for operating purposes as a means of individual train identification, was in transition; eventually leading to the modern form of four digit codes. Until 18th June 1962 the standard train classification headlamp codes had been classed by alphabetical letters from 'A to K'. In order to facilitate the transition to the four digit system these required to be changed to a numerical sequence from '1 to 10' (10 being expressed as zero). So, depending on the date of the picture the train is either a 'Class H,' or in the new format, 'Class 8' freight. As with many of the '9F's, '92248's' life was but a short one. It was withdrawn on 13th June 1965 after just six years and six months service and 'cut-up' at Cashmore's Yard, Newport two months later. *GH1309*

Image 114: Only a few yards further north from the previous Image 113 but a full decade earlier; just look at the contrast in the condition of the two locomotives. Undoubtedly Engine Common was another favourite location that George continued to return to over the years. In this photograph 'Jubilee Class' 45626 'Seychelles' scoots south at the head of a twelve coach cross-country express. All of the coaches except the second and third appear to be of 'BR Mark 1' design. Such coaches were being introduced during the early part of the 1950's. The locomotive's shed code plate looks suspiciously like Derby (17A) substantiating that this is probably a North-East to West of England express which the engine would have taken over at Derby. It was a time when labour was still cheap and pride was taken in the presentation of express locomotives. 'Seychelles' was based at Derby from June 1951 until November 1961, by which time these trains were beginning to be taken over by 'Peak Class' diesels. During this period a number of these heavy inter-regional cross-country trains ran between Newcastle and West Yorkshire to Bristol and the West so without any particular indication it would be difficult to pinpoint the particular train. But as an example a regular train throughout the decade was the midday from Newcastle leaving at various times between noon and 1.00pm arriving at Temple Meads in the late afternoon/early evening. The lighting in this photograph seems to fit this train admirably. *GH0301*

Left Image 115: This is a real period piece and may rank as one of George's earliest photographs. It captures one of the 738 ex-Midland Railway 'Class 4F' locomotives originally designed by Henry Fowler in 1911. Plodding south at Engine Common north of Yate with, according to its headlamp code, a 'Class H' unfitted freight, is '4169' which has a tender still labelled 'LMS'. Behind the tender is a series of wagons ranging from coal to an assortment of sheeted trucks and is probably a Gloucester (Barnwood) to Westerleigh Yard, Bristol St. Philip's or Stoke Gifford goods train. For such a humble train the engine '4169' appears to be in an incredibly clean and well presented condition. Thanks to the freely available records of the Stephenson Locomotive Society there is strong evidence that this engine carried its ex-LMS identification well into post nationalisation days. On 28th February 1950, a Society member noted '4169' entering Derby Works for an overhaul. Whilst in the Works it was officially re-numbered '44169' on 11th March 1950. On 28th April 1950 it was again noted having been repainted and ready for release but with its tender still displaying the 'LMS' lettering. At this time the engine was allocated to Barrow Road (22A). Whilst all this is circumstantial evidence it nevertheless gives an indication of the period of the photograph and why '44169' is in such condition. Originally '4169' had been released into service in March 1926 from Crewe Works. It continued in service right through until August 1965 when it was withdrawn from Buxton (9L) after 39 years and 6 months service; a true testimony to its durability. *GH1350*

Bottom Image 116: This picture is a beautiful representation of bucolic England during the middle of the twentieth century; the cattle are being herded across the bridge back to the farm for milking. The difference here is that all the vegetation is in full bloom and the crows nests in the trees are fully dressed by nature for the protection of the birds and their offspring. The cows look like Holstein Friesians, a breed of dairy cattle that originated in the Dutch provinces of North Holland and Friesland, and Schleswig-Holstein in Northern Germany. They are known as the world's highest-producing dairy animals and the Gloucestershire countryside provided rich pasture. Through this idyll another Fowler 'Class 4F' 43989 coasts south with what is probably the same train as in the previous image (115) but a number of years later. It was based at Bournville (21B) from the autumn of 1954 to the summer 1958 when re-allocated to Burton (17B) until it was withdrawn on 23rd April 1960. It had entered service from Derby Works in 1921. The LMS went on to construct 530 of the locomotives between 1923 and 1928. A further 45 examples were reluctantly authorised by William Stanier in 1937 at the behest of the operating department. Amongst many keen trainspotters of the 1950's they were known as 'Duck Sixes', a reference to their rather inelegant look and six-coupled wheel arrangement. *GH1356*

Image 117: It probably isn't good practice to present a number of pictures all taken from virtually the same position, but when they represent the changing face of the railways over the course of a decade they cannot be denied. Such was George's determination to record this change that he continued to return to this particular spot, not least for its photogenicity. It began with Image 115 and this set of four photographs, all taken from virtually the same position, show interesting comparisons in the settings, seasons and make up of different trains. In this example, another picture taken at much the same time as Image 115, during the very early years of the 1950's. A southbound local passenger train gallops from beneath the bridge at Engine Common headed by a 'Class 4P' 40934; one of the post- grouping developments of Samuel Johnson's 3-cylinder Midland Railway Compound locomotives. It was one of seventy five such engines built at Vulcan Foundry, Newton-le-Willows and put into service during June 1927. It was allocated to Gloucester (Barnwood) (22B) from November 1952 until its withdrawal in March 1957. One of the Class, '41000' was preserved and restored to its Midland maroon livery and given its original number '1000'. It is in the National Collection and is believed to currently be on loan to the Scottish Railway Preservation Society at Bo'ness as a static exhibit. *GH1422*

Image 118: Now a late 1950's photograph; where the same bridge carries a rural lane over the railway at Engine Common, George has cajoled a friend into throwing a jocular wave from the line-side as the train passes. The fireman leans out of his cab staring ahead obliviously. The locomotive, 'Black Five' 44802, trundles south with a train that appears to be a summer extra from the north carrying a London Midland Region 'TRN' that cannot be clearly distinguished. Between February 1948 and May 1958 '44802' was allocated to Sheffield Grimesthorpe (19B). The train comprises some ageing stock. The leading vehicle is a 'Diagram 960 PMV'; one of a series of Parcels and Miscellaneous Vans built by the South Eastern and Chatham Railway from 1919. The Southern Railway continued to build similar vehicles and further batches were built by BR until 1951. Some of these vehicles continued to be used into the 1980's. The next two coaches are both ex LNER composite coaches designed by Nigel Gresley in 1923. Using a 60ft underframe these coaches had a wooden teak-panelled body with square mouldings and windows and varnished teak livery. The LNER continued to construct them until 1942. By the late 1950's they were appearing in different colours, the first coach is in Crimson Lake and Cream (Blood and Custard) introduced by BR in 1949. Is the coach beneath the bridge still in its ageing teak livery or is it painted in the later maroon livery introduced from May 1956, it's difficult to say? The last of these type of coaches were not withdrawn until 1965. *GH1334*

Image 119: This photograph is taken from the bridge itself and could be entitled 'Clear Road Ahead'. A somewhat neglected 'BR Standard Class 5' forges north with an express from Temple Meads. The clear road is demonstrated by the Rangeworthy Distant signal ahead which is in the 'off' position. So the engine, showing a clean exhaust, has steam full on and gallops along on the falling gradient. The post holding the Yate 'Down' Distant signal is to the right of the engine's tender. It is clearly late autumn or early winter, the trees have shed their leaves and the grasses on the embankment are now just golden in the late afternoon light. The sun is waning and the long shadows of trees rest on the leading carriage; George has painted a great autumnal picture. It again epitomises the standard to which railway infrastructure was kept sixty plus years ago; the substantial stone built platelayer's hut, just to the fore of the engine, has now been consigned to history. The condition of the locomotive suggests this picture was taken in the latter days of steam. The time of year and the weak sunlight give a clue as to which train this may be. Using the 1963 LMR public time table as an example, the two contenders would be the 1.40pm ex-Temple Meads to York or the 2.40pm ex-Temple Meads to Nottingham Midland. Each would be passing this location about twenty five minutes after leaving Bristol. *GH0709*

Image 120: This photograph was probably taken on the same occasion as that featured in 'Atmospheric Western' (Image 71). But for this photograph George has manoeuvred his wife Shirley and son Richard into a position in front of the tree which still remains central to his composition. Here he now captures an 'Up' fast freight in the hands of a 'Jubilee' locomotive. If this picture was taken post-1960 this is likely to be a Class 4 or 5, (express fitted freight); the difference being that a Class 4 had the vacuum brake fitted to not less than ninety per cent of the vehicles whereas a Class 5 had the automatic brake fitted to not less than half of the vehicles, giving it less braking power and thus time-tabled at a lesser speed. With this train's consist of vacuum fitted vans and early container flat wagons (conflats) which were also vacuum fitted, makes this more likely to be the former. These designations changed during 1960/61 when headlamp codes were reclassified into numerical codes rather than letter which would probably have made this then a 'Class C' freight pre-1960. Again we are deep in the Gloucestershire open countryside and the hay has been baled in the field beyond the railway. It is a lovely evening and a joy to be out in such surroundings with the Cotswold village of Wotton-under-Edge in the background together with a landmark geographical feature placed directly above the Charfield Distant signal. This 111ft. high tower was raised in 1866 to commemorate William Tyndale, born locally, who risked his life to bring us the Christian Bible in everyday language that ordinary people could understand. In 1535, as a result of his views, he was burned at the stake. *GH0636*

Image 121: It appears to be a mellow late afternoon or early autumn evening as 'Jubilee' 45631 'Tanganyika', breezing along with safety valves open, passes the Rangeworthy 'Up' Distant signal approaching Hall End with a 'Class 5' freight. This was 'an express freight train with the automatic brake operative on not fewer than half of the vehicles' This would suggest that the open wagon, five back from the engine, would have been vacuum pipe fitted. In the background just in front of the over-bridge at Engine Common the Yate Main Line Junction 'Down' Distant has been pulled off ready to accept a train. The fascinating feature of this photograph is 'Tanganyika' displaying a shed code plate carrying a single numeral and letter. The record of 'Tanganyika's' allocations disclose that this would probably be Saltley (By then 2E) where, in her twilight years, according to SLS records she spent a short spell between March 1963 and August 1964. Those dates give a very narrow window during which this picture could have been taken. It also confirms this train as a 'Class 5 'freight. Within a week of being re-allocated to Crewe North (5A) in August 1964 she had been condemned and withdrawn from service. Many a young trainspotter of the period learned much about world geography from their hobby; 'Tanganyika' was formerly one of Britain's colonies in Africa, now better known as Tanzania. *GH1219*

Opposite Top Image 122: Another mile further on as we approach the Rangeworthy area, the railway is crossed by a road bridge which carries a country lane connecting Leechpool with Yate Lower Common. It is here George spotted the opportunity to use the arch of the bridge as a frame for his photograph. Entering into that frame, which becomes a portrait, trundles a 'Black Five' 44843 with a southbound heavy train of pulverised coal. Having climbed the 1 in 281 gradient from before Charfield up to Rangeworthy signal box the crew have a moment to relax on a level stretch of track. The safety valves are just feathering so the fire is in good order. The engine is displaying a 'Class 8' (unfitted freight) headlamp code. Based at Saltley (21A) from July 1963 until June 1965 '44843' was noted, on 9th February 1964, in the Erecting Shop at Crewe Works, which infers it was probably undergoing an overhaul. Although suffering some kind of leak from around the top of the boiler the engine still looks in otherwise clean condition which may reflect that visit to Crewe. Traditionally on steam locomotives the uppermost lamp bracket was carried at the top of the smoke box door but on this engine that position has been changed to the nearside hinged part of the door on this locomotive, which may have been effected during that overhaul. Latterly this change was applied to a number of locomotives probably for operational reasons, not least of which, was for the fireman, having to place the headlamp in position beneath overhead electric wires. *GH1361*

Image 123 Bottom: As with preceding images in this album it may be considered unusual to place two pictures, both taken from exactly the same place, alongside one another. But in order to display George's artistic instincts the resulting effect is self evident, which further emphasises the fact that he was 'A Man for All Seasons'. The first picture is clearly taken on an early autumn evening; the trees are still in full leaf and the field has been mown. George has persuaded Shirley to go down into the field and as the shadows of a fine evening lengthen, stand amongst the stubble to watch the 7.25pm Bristol to Newcastle mail train race north. Headed by an unidentified 'Jubilee' (or is it a 'Standard Class 5'?) the train comprises six BR Mark 1 coaches with the TPO vehicles trailing behind. All three of the Post Office vehicles appear to be dated to the early 1930's. When introduced by the LMS, the middle one, a 60ft sorting carriage, shows the position where the automatic collecting apparatus would have originally been stowed, towards the rear. The 7.25pm departure from Temple Meads was a long term arrangement with the Post Office. It had formed a connection there with the Great Western 'North Mail' which left Plymouth at 3.45pm after picking up traffic and through coaches from the noon departure ex-Penzance. With calls at Newton Abbot, Exeter and Taunton that train was due to arrive at Temple Meads at 7.00pm. The laborious journey of this train culminated with an arrival at Newcastle at 4.31am, although passengers could arrive earlier at 4.16am by changing onto an alternative service at York, still representing a journey of over sixteen hours from Penzance. *GH0370*

Image 124: Moving from the warmth of a summer evening the second picture starkly contrasts the same scene in deep mid-winter. It must have taken some grit on George's part to drive out from home to a small country lane in the heart of rural Gloucestershire in such conditions with the hope of getting a good photograph. The ground is blanketed in snow and in the sky it looks as though there is more to come. But his effort was worth it, capturing this photograph of what appears to be a 'BR Standard Class 5' pressing onward through this winter wonderland with a Temple Meads to Birmingham express. The landmark in the background which marries the two pictures together is a very substantial farm. This is Hall End Farmhouse. It is an early 17th Century building, remodelled in 1688, standing on a medieval site. It was Grade II listed in September 1952. Note that some of the windows on the train are open; either the train is carrying few passengers or those on board are very hardy souls. There were two memorable 'whiteout' Christmas and New Year periods during the early 1960's. In 1961 the run up to the New Year introduced heavy snowfalls with depths of snow reaching 12-16 inches, giving a white New Year to many places. The following year was far worse. Significant snowfall began on Boxing Day and cold air became firmly established. The big freeze began. As then a callow youth, the writer recalls, returning to London by train from Shrewsbury in such conditions after a Christmas break at home. I remember travelling through a cutting somewhere in the vicinity of Haddenham in the Chilterns and all that could be seen out of the carriage window was a sheer wall of snow; I believe this was reported to be the first train on the line to get through since Christmas. A thaw did not begin until 6th March. This picture could have been taken during either winter. *GH0707*

Image 125: Everything in this picture is similar to Images 123 and 124 except the direction of the train. The time of year looks the same as Image 123, even though the evening sunlight differs slightly. The slender figure appearing in Image 123, George's long suffering wife, has now wandered further into the distance to watch another Caprotti fitted 'Black Five' coasting past with its eleven coach express bound for Bristol. Most of the carriages in the train's make up are BR Mark 1 coaches or of ex-LMS origin, particularly those at three and four behind the tender where the kitchen and restaurant car facilities are situated. Their work almost complete the kitchen car staff must be clearing up as the train is not far from journey's end. It is coasting along here on a level section of track before it meets a slight rise towards Yate. The safety valves are just feathering in readiness, so with the boiler ready, the driver has time to look out to appreciate the countryside; it must be running on time. The locomotive's number is difficult to read but the only Caprotti fitted 'Black-Five' in the group of numbers deciphered makes '44753' the most likely. This engine went newly built to Holbeck (20A) on 27th March 1948 and remained there until early November 1963. Its condition suggests this may be an early 1960's view and during that period the only express having a Restaurant Car and passing this point in the evening was the 12.15pm Newcastle to Plymouth due to arrive at Temple Meads at 6.56pm. The Leeds engine and the front portion including the Dining Cars would be taken off there and the rest of the train would then proceed on to Plymouth behind a Western Region locomotive. *GH1397*

Image 126: The next point we come to is Rangeworthy Signal Box. As can be seen from its **ARP** design, this box was a **WWII** introduction opened on 25th January 1942. The reason was to break the block section between **Charfield** and **Wickwar** in half and subsequently introduce a crossover for operational exigencies. It is here on a balmy summer afternoon that George recorded another 'Stanier Black Five' 44917 coasting south, carrying an **LMR** 'TRN' 'W196', which regrettably we are unable to identify. The second coach appears to be carrying a carriage headboard which may suggest it is a regular train as distinct to a summer extra. This locomotive was posted to Bath (Green Park) from February 1952 until June 1958. During 1958 a regional boundary of the Somerset and Dorset Railway was drawn at Templecombe and the northern section was transferred from the **LMR** to the Western Region. Historically this was the beginning of the end for the **S & D**. So in the early summer of 1958 could this Green Park allocated engine carrying an **LMR** 'TRN' with a Western Region destination code be bound for the **S & D**? There is a point for discussion. *GH1426*

Image 127: Clearly George had developed a relationship with the signalmen at Rangeworthy Box and took a number of photographs from and around it. On an earlier occasion but from the other side of the box he captured a 'Fowler 4F' 43946 approaching Hardwicke Level Crossing, alternatively known as Hall End Crossing, through a plethora of signs immediately north of the box. This was an occupation crossing on the original alignment of the Yate to Wickwar road which was diverted when the line was built in 1845. Hardwicke Farm cottages can be seen behind the elevated Rangeworthy home signal protecting the crossing. '43946' is galloping along on the slightly rising gradient of 1 in 281 with a 'Class J' goods, then classified as a mineral or empty wagon train. This sprightly looking engine was based at Saltley (21A) from prior to nationalisation on 1st January 1948 until July 1956 when it was reallocated north to Toton (18A) and then further north to Staveley (Barrow Hill) (41E). It was noted by an **SLS** correspondent in April 1950 as entering Derby Works for an overhaul, still carrying its old **LMS** Number '3946'. This photograph then must have been taken during the first half of the decade and very probably soon after this overhaul. Particularly note, on the extreme left the sign which reads 'Beware of Trains; Stop, Look, Listen'. In addition to the signs relating to the crossing the prominent Temporary Speed Restriction sign on the 'Up' line indicates that relaying or re-ballasting has taken or is due to take place. *GH1423*

Image 128: This is followed by a similar photograph but this time taken from out of the box. Here a very clean 'Stanier Black Five' traverses Hardwicke Level Crossing and has a clear road south with a 'Class C' train of perishables, running under passenger train timings. '44853' was released from Crewe Works in November 1944 and appears to have gone straight to Leeds (Holbeck) (20A) and remained there throughout its career until its withdrawal in June 1967. In this picture we have a much clearer view of the type of crossing this was. On the 28th June 1949 at 5.55pm what might have been a catastrophic accident occurred here. The 5.15pm Bristol to Birmingham 'Up' ordinary stopping train, travelling at about 50mph collided with a private motor car. As a result the engine, an ex-Midland 'Class 4P' 4-4-0 hauling five coaches, became derailed and carried the car in front of it for a further 140 yards before the car fell down the slight embankment. The engine received only superficial damage but the car, a 1935 model 10 H.P. Austin Saloon was wrecked. Remarkably the occupant, the wife of the owner of the farm served by the crossing, escaped with cuts, bruises and severe shock; there were no other casualties. The report of Colonel D. McMullen, the Ministry of Transport's Inquiring Officer makes fascinating reading. As is often the case in railway accidents the cause was human error when everything that could go wrong conspired to go wrong all at the same time. The remarkable thing is that this Crossing, only some twenty or thirty yards north of the box, had no physical connection with it. The Temporary Speed Restriction sign in both photographs suggest this picture was taken at much the same time as the previous image. Note in the 'four foot', in front of the engine, rail lengths have been stored in readiness for relaying. *GH1417*

Image 129: This photograph is taken from the realigned road referred to in Image 128, from just about the point where the car in the 1949 accident came to rest. The locomotive ploughed on for another 360 yards. In this picture the evening sun lights an unidentified 'Black Five' and the leading full brake van of its 'Down' train, likely an express or parcels. Whilst the Reporting Officer conducting the Inquiry into the accident largely placed the blame on the car driver, poor Mrs Hardwicke, he did place on record "It is regrettable that when constructed, Rangeworthy signal box was not set further back so as to avoid obstruction to the view of the 'Up' line…" He also recommended raising the height of the 'Up' signal so that it is visible above the box from the 'Up' side gate. His final recommendation was the installation of "Stop, Look, Listen" notices in positions conspicuous to road users. This photograph amply illustrates the closeness of the box to the line and the elevated home signals on both sides. Perhaps it was this accident which had a bearing on the increased introduction of "Stop, Look, Listen" boards displayed at footpath and occupation crossings across the country. Note the ghostly form in the signal box; is this the panel or is it the signalman, the owner of the Ford Saloon car parked at the rear of the box? *GH1415*

Image 130: The reason for the Temporary Permanent Way Slack (Images 127 & 128) now becomes apparent. This is where track relaying was being carried out, just north of Rangeworthy. Almost dating back a century, it remained very labour intensive but was soon to be overtaken by mechanisation (See Image 89).The first picture illustrates how the work was still being carried out. George must have had advanced notice of these works which were generally undertaken on a Sunday. Both pictures were taken from the West End lane road over bridge; the first bridge north of Rangeworthy. Beneath the engine the new length of rail has been laid. The 'Fowler 4F' has just started slowly pulling the ballast hoppers over the new length with a man controlling the slow release from each hopper as the engine moves backwards. One or two supervisors stand with hands clasped behind their backs while the labourers wait with shovels at the ready. *GH1313*

Image 131: The second image is taken from the same position so it can now be established exactly where we are with Hardwicke Farm Cottages in the background and the train in the distance in the vicinity of Rangeworthy signal box. In this image the result of the 'dropping crew' may be seen, the ballast has been evenly distributed along the length and the work of spreading and packing the ballast between and beneath the sleepers has commenced. These men are in for a long and arduous afternoon completing this task. Clearly single line working is in operation, note the 'Lookout' standing on the 'Up' side line about a quarter of a mile away. His job was to ensure the safety of the relaying gang and when he saw a train approaching sounded a horn to inform them of its approach. He would have a counterpart a similar distance away to the north. This was the extent of Health and Safety during this period. Note also the 'T' Board on the 'Down' side in the middle distance. This sign indicated to an engine driver the termination of a temporary speed restriction; perhaps rather premature in the light of the photographic evidence. *GH1362*

Image 132: Taken from the other side of the bridge carrying the diverted lane, on a glorious summer evening, George captures an ex-GWR '2800 class' 2-8-0 'Heavy Freight' engine heading south with a 'Class H' unfitted freight, epitomised by the mixed types of seemingly loaded coal wagons, which take up the first two-thirds of the train. In fact the engine is a 'Class 2884', a Charles Collett development of the design. These differed from the original engines in a number of respects, the most obvious being that a more modern side window cab was provided and that they were built with outside steam pipes. From a grainy enlargement of the photograph the smoke box number plate looks suspiciously like '3823'. This engine entered service from Swindon in May 1940 but more importantly, in the context of this picture, was allocated to Severn Tunnel Junction (86E) from August 1955 to May 1958. If that was the case then this would possibly be a Severn Tunnel Junction to Westerleigh Sidings or more likely Stoke Gifford Yard freight, many such heavy slow moving trains were sent this way to avoid delaying other traffic through the busy Severn Tunnel. It looks as though the driver has spotted the photographer and called his mate over to become part of the picture. The bucolic nature of the countryside is emphasised by the dairy cattle grazing in the surrounding fields. After further service at Southall, Oxford and Neath '3823' subsequently returned to Severn Tunnel Junction in November 1964 and was withdrawn eight months later. *GH0629*

Image 133: Taken from adjacent to the bridge in the background of the previous Image 132 we have now returned to the early 1950's. This was another favoured location George discovered fairly early in his photographic ventures, about six miles' cycle ride from his home, just right for an evening ride after a days work. It is here, beside a substantial road over-bridge, he recorded this scene of another ex-Midland Railway 'Class 4P' (Compound) locomotive 41073 coasting north with a local train; next stop Wickwar (7.9pm). An **SLS** correspondent noted this engine entering Derby Works in March 1950 still bearing its LMS number '1073' By the end of April it was again noted, in the same Works, by a further **SLS** report as being 'painted black and fully lined, with the **BR** crest. Subsequently, in November 1955, it was again noted in the Erecting Shop at Derby for another overhaul. With the engine in this photograph looking in such good condition this picture could have been taken shortly after either event. '41073' was based at Bournville (21B), a Birmingham depot, right through from Nationalisation until it was withdrawn in August 1957. The six ex-LMS corridor coaches with two vans at the rear, seems too strong a train just to be running between Bristol and Gloucester. With an evening atmosphere in the picture and in the knowledge that the locomotive was based at Birmingham the deduction has to be this train is probably the 6.30pm Temple Meads to New Street which would be passing this point at about five minutes past seven. *GH1442*

Image 134: Evenings in rural Gloucestershire seems to have been one of George's preferences. Marginally further north and with steam shut off 'Castle' 5010 'Restormel Castle' coasts down the 1 in 281 grade just south of Wickwar Tunnel passing Hall End. A Train Reporting Number has been hastily scrawled across the smoke box door which is barely legible, apart from the first figure to the left of the smoke box number plate which appears is a '6' but the other two numbers are open to conjecture. 'Restormel Castle' was based at Stafford Road (84A) from May 1950 until March 1958, except for a brief two month posting to Laira (83D) during early 1953, so the train's destination is fairly clear. The fact that the number is hastily applied is once again an indication that this was perhaps an additional one arranged at short notice. The train's make up consists of a mixture of differently designed coaches which adds to the prospect. However, the fourth vehicle behind the tender is either a restaurant or buffet car which indicates the train to be a more regular one. This probably means that it is the engine that has been a late addition to the train, being commandeered at the last moment to perhaps cover for a failure of the rostered engine on shed. Close examination of the photograph reveals that the 'Down' line has been re-laid using flat bottom rail whereas the 'Up' track is still laid using the traditional bullhead type. *GH0605*

Image 135: This picture is taken from West End Lane bridge looking south and once again Shirley has taken a position 'right of stage' to give balance and a form of introduction leading the eye into the picture. Also, again, it is a late summer/early autumn picture; the grasses in the foreground are fully grown and Mrs. Heiron is still wearing a summer dress. In the background is Hall End Lane Bridge and, to the left, are the outbuildings of Hall End Farm. All the coaches in view are BR Mark 1's and painted in maroon livery. From 1956 the separate Regions were given the option of returning to their pre-nationalisation colours. The London Midland, Eastern and Scottish Regions all adopted this maroon livery which strongly resembled that of the former LMS. Economic reasons dictated liveries usually being changed piecemeal, when coaches came in for scheduled maintenance or in the case of later Mark 1's, as they were released into service. This 'Jubilee' still looks reasonably well turned out. It is suggested that this picture would have been taken towards the turn of the decade. In the 1960 Western Region summer timetable the 12.43pm ex-Newcastle was due at Temple Meads at 8.20pm meaning it would be passing this point at about 7.45pm which seems to fit with the light and shade of the photograph. *GH1311*

Image 136: We are still at the same location but in this picture we are looking north on the upside of the line with George crouching at rail level just in front of the P. Way hut seen in Images 133, 134 and 135. The result is this imposing view of a very smart 'Jubilee' 45610 gliding south with an express for Bristol. '45610' was released into service from Crewe Works on 19th July, 1934 carrying its original name 'Gold Coast'. At the time of nationalisation it was allocated to Derby (17A) and for the larger part of its service this is one of the principal routes it worked. It was still based at Derby when it was withdrawn on 11th June 1964. The Gold Coast declared its independence from Britain on 6th March 1957 and renamed itself Ghana. This new name for its former colony was subsequently recognised by the British government. 'Gold Coast' was renamed 'Ghana' in 1958, as a consequence. The name board in this picture appears to carry two words rather than one suggesting this picture being taken prior to the name change. The leading vehicle behind the tender is a BR Mark 1 BSK followed by what appear to be two ex-GWR coaches, the second of which is a Dining/Buffet Car. And what is going on in the foreground? It appears concrete trunking is being laid in readiness for cabling to be introduced for the installation of automatic colour light signalling. The substantial permanent way hut with its sharpening wheel for scythe and sickle is still a throwback to the days of a 'lengthman' whose job it was to maintain a certain length of track and trackside. All these indicators suggest an early 1950's decade photograph. *GH0277*

Image 137: Although we are still in the same area as Image 135 the viewpoint differs. That shot was taken from the bridge whereas this picture embraces it. Another very atmospheric Heiron view records the lingering exhaust of a 'Down' Freight train still hanging in the air. The bridge in the foreground carries a lane connecting the small communities of Hall End and West End. The heavy freight, quite likely a 'Class H', headed by what appears to be a 'Stanier 8F' is mostly made up of loaded coal wagons, a number of vans and sheeted wagons. Some of the coal wagons carry lump coal, probably for locomotives, whilst others contain pulverised coal for power station or other industrial use. The train's destination could be Westerleigh Yard or more likely Stoke Gifford. It is about to meet a Bristol to Birmingham express headed by what looks like a 'Jubilee' or 'Black Five'. The long grasses and wild flowers indicate it is late summer and the bales of hay in the fields show the grain has been harvested. A feature of this photograph is the three aspect colour light signal immediately in front of the bridge. This was probably the point where the Rangeworthy 'Down' distant signal had previously been situated. This type of Colour Light signalling was the basic introduction of a type which led to the demise of semaphore signalling and the eventual abolition of Rangeworthy Signal Box. It was closed on 19th October 1969. *GH1342*

Image 138: A classic Heiron pin sharp photograph of a pristine ex-GW 'Grange Class' 6871 'Bourton Grange' speeding out of the south end of Wickwar Tunnel with a 'Class 3' parcels train. The locomotive's presentation could deceive one into believing this picture would have been taken much earlier than it actually was. However close inspection of the smoke box door reveals the engine's shed code to be 2B. 'Bourton Grange' had been re-allocated from Llanelly (87F) to Oxley (then 84B) during the early autumn of 1960. However on 1st January 1963, due to Western Region boundary changes, Oxley had been transferred to the London Midland Region and subsequently became 2B from 1st September. Whilst these changes were taking place '6871' was noted on 24th March in Stafford Road Works at Wolverhampton undergoing an overhaul. Putting this information together suggests this photograph would have perhaps been taken during early autumn 1963. The train itself was likely to be a 'Parcels' from the West Midlands to Bristol. 'Bourton Grange' was again noted in 'A' shop at Swindon Works undergoing further attention in April 1964. She was eventually withdrawn from service only eighteen months later on 16th October 1965 and went to Cohen's Yard at Kettering where she was cut up during March 1966. It is a matter of great regret that not even a single 'Grange' was rescued for preservation but had it been, surely 'Bourton Grange' would have been a prime candidate. By way of compensation, a newly built 'Grange' 6880 'Betton Grange', the' 81st of the Class, is currently under construction. *GH1330*

Image 139 Opposite Top: At a slightly higher elevation we are still in the deep cutting at the south end of Wickwar Tunnel where George staged this photograph to include a friend throwing up a jocular salute to the crew of ex-Midland 'Class 4F' 43946 clambering out of the tunnel on a 1 in 281 rising gradient, with a Bristol bound 'Class D' partly fitted express freight. The driver fails to respond, dutifully looking ahead. Is this the same man as the one we saw earlier in Image 118, the stance is almost the same? '43946' is appearing very trim with its smoke box looking polished and a very distinguishing '21A' shed plate. This engine was built for the Midland Railway by Armstrong Whitworth and released into service in 1921. It had been allocated to Saltley (21A) during the late 1940's and was noted by an SLS correspondent entering Derby Works for an overhaul on 30th April 1950, carrying its LMS number '3946'. It must have been during this works visit that its British Railways number was first applied. The engine's appearance may therefore suggest this picture being taken during the early part of the decade. The durability and versatility of this class of locomotive is perfectly demonstrated in this photograph of a thirty years plus old engine still being deployed on a long distance mainline fast freight. The 1,401 yards long Wickwar Tunnel, which had longstanding flooding and associated problems, opened at the same time as the Bristol and Gloucester Railway in 1844. It was originally engineered by Isambard Kingdom Brunel to accommodate the broad gauge but with the almost immediate take-over of the B & G by the Midland Railway, was laid to standard gauge. *GH0034*

Image 140 Below: At the other end of the tunnel a 'Jubilee' 45662 'Kempenfelt' hoves into view with the 'Up' Devonian showing very little steam, having coasted through the tunnel, now emerging into the confines of Wickwar station. Her impressive presentation suggests a recent overhaul. The first two coaches are both of ex-LMS design so we must be looking at a mid decade photograph. To the left, the former Brewery siding is now weed strewn. With brewing having long since ceased at the Brewery the requirement for rail access was no longer needed but the connection remained purely for operational needs as seen in following images. Once again the view from rail level makes for a very impressive picture and must have been taken during much the same time as the following Image 141. In a WTT of the period the weekday 'Up Devonian', 9.15am Paignton to Bradford was scheduled to pass Yate South Junction at 12.59pm and Charfield seven minutes later, 1.6pm. On summer Saturdays these timings were changed when the train started from Kingswear at 8.45am. This meant it was due to pass the former at 12.39pm and the latter eleven minutes later (including three minutes recovery time) at 12.50pm. The recovery time provided for congestion and/or operating difficulties. Either time meant the train would be approaching Wickwar just before one o'clock. *GH1318*

Image 141: Another iconic Heiron photograph, one of the compiler's favourite pictures; George appears to have inveigled the entire Wickwar station staff to stand and salute the passage of an 'Up' Bristol to Birmingham express. On parade on the signal box balcony are, according to their respective uniforms, the station master, porter and with his head out of the window; the Wickwar signalman. Viewed from rail level we have quite a dramatic action shot of an immaculate 'Jubilee Class 6P5F' 4-6-0 45662 'Kempenfelt', this time roaring through. With regulator open she is taking full advantage of the falling gradient onwards to Charfield. The haze emitting from the tunnel shrouds the background. As we saw earlier 'Kempenfelt' was a long term resident of Barrow Road (22A) from, at least, 1948 right through until October 1961 when her express duties were usurped by 'Peak' Diesels. Here she is in immaculate condition; a credit to the Barrow Road cleaners. The first coach behind the tender is an ex-LMS Period 1 coach from the late 1920's; the others visible are also ex-LMS but of a later flush sided design introduced by William Stanier, probably dating the picture to the first years of the decade. On the left is the very substantial building of Wickwar Brewery. In the foreground is some very intricate track work associated with the Goods Shed. The winds of change are afoot. At this stage the loop appears still to be in use, occupied by a Brake Van and some trucks. *GH1320*

Image 142: For this photograph George must have taken up a position high up on the embankment midway between the Brewery and the tunnel to allow him to take photographs of trains entering and leaving the tunnel. The result is this picture of 'Jubilee' 45572 'Eire' entering, heading a Bristol bound express with '**BRITISH RAILWAYS**' conspicuously displayed on its tender. This title was the first emblem introduced after nationalisation on 1st January 1948 and was carried by many locomotives and numerous classes, lasting, at least officially, until the arrival in 1949 of the first lion and wheel emblem, or totem as it was known. The last time we saw 'Eire' was in Image 88 but in that photograph, probably taken a couple of years later, she was by then sporting that lion and wheel on her tender. There is evidence here of forthcoming engineering works, all the wooden sleepers lying in the 'four-foot' of the headshunt are new. And the intricate crossover point-work in the adjacent 'four-foot', beside the 'Down' main line, re-enforces this. The early lettering on the tender, taken together with the relaying track work and sleepers strewn around, suggest this picture was probably taken at much the same time as the previous photograph. 'Eire' is on record as entering Crewe Works for overhaul on 30th January 1949, probably prior to the lion and wheel emblem becoming officially approved and was out-shopped carrying this lettering. Hence the dating of this photograph is to the very early 1950's. *GH1364*

Image 143: From much the same position as the previous photograph George has now turned his camera around and on the right we can see the tower of Wickwar Brewery and beyond is the Goods Shed. Speeding through the station is an unidentified ex GWR 'Hall' Class locomotive with its copper capped chimney and brass safety valve cover still in good order. It displays a TRN '823' that in the summer timetables of 1956, 1957 and 1958 applied to the 10.55am (SO) Birmingham to Paignton, which gives us a time frame for the picture. The engine for the working during this period would probably have been supplied by Tyseley (84E). This was the principal shed serving Birmingham but the largest passenger engines allocated there were the 'Halls', of which the engine in this shot is probably one. The reason for this was that all the principal Western Region expresses worked to and from Wolverhampton rather than Birmingham. Tyseley always had a good allocation of 'Halls', seventeen in 1950 but reduced to nine by 1959. In the following year the originating station of this train had been moved back to Wolverhampton (Low Level) with a start time at 10.35am. At the same time the train was re-designated as TRN '334'. This photograph may well have been taken at the same time as Image 140; note the rails lying beside the 'Down' line are all in exactly the same position. The 'Temporary Speed Restriction Post' adjacent to the engine also adds to the scenario. *GH1185*

Image 144: It was in the early 1950's that George must have had permission from the owners of the Brewery to climb to the top of the tower seen in the previous Image 143. It is from here we have a bird's eye view of an unidentified 'Black Five' coasting out of the tunnel with a Birmingham bound express. This again is probably a summer extra; the 'TRN' is being carried in the middle of the buffer beam rather than at the top of the smokebox door. The first three coaches all appear to be of Stanier flush sided stock. But the roof of the fourth coach carries ventilator equipment indicating a restaurant/dining car. There are also wagons sitting beside the Brewery dock, two empty open wagons and a van with its sliding door open. A recently built cycle shed and another corrugated building indicate the site is still in full use. The Wickwar Brewery opened in 1800 and was listed as a Company by Thomas Arnold who died in 1853. In about 1886 a new brewery was built near the station to replace the original at 34 High Street. With the construction of this new brewery it is probably safe to assume that the Brewery siding was opened at the same time. In 1887 Arnold's merged with Perrett's of Wotton-under-Edge to become Arnold, Perrett & Co. Ltd. with 325 locally tied houses. A further merger in 1924 led to brewing ceasing at the plant but the premises continued to be used as a cider factory until 1969-70. *GH1322*

Image 145: One might be confused into thinking this is a railway in miniature. George found a wonderful viewpoint on a hillside to the north of the village to record this scene of an unidentified 'Black Five' cruising along on the falling gradient towards Charfield with an eleven coach express for the Midlands and the North. Its smoke haze is still emitting from the tunnel mouth. Just passing the Wickwar 'Up' home starter signal, the train is made up of largely ex-LMS coaching stock with the fourth vehicle being a Restaurant Car. The road it is crossing is that to Wotton-under-Edge. With the newly built house on the right, together with a large greenhouse and orchard it looks as if a market gardening business is being set up. Towards the background, alongside this road the station building and Goods shed can be seen and beyond that the tall building is the Brewery. This building still survives and in 1990 brewing recommenced under the title of Wickwar Brewing Company. Alas in 2021 it closed once more, brewing being contracted out elsewhere. The village itself sits on the hill in the background and to the right overlooking it is the tall tower of the seven hundred years old Holy Trinity Parish Church. Goods services were withdrawn from Wickwar in 1963 and for passengers, with the withdrawal of stopping trains between Bristol and Gloucester, in 1965. *GH1358*

Image 146: It is an English high summer day on the edge of the Cotswolds. We are now at Huntingford just a mile or two north of Charfield. The 'Down' Charfield distant signal is in the background. Clearly, the 'length' has recently been re-laid; the ballast is pristine and the surplus spread along the 'Up' side embankment parallel with the rails. Such pride in the job is rarely recorded but is exemplified in this picture. Through this scene an unidentified '70xx series Castle Class' locomotive, possibly 7026 'Tenby Castle' hastens west with 'TRN 825' 'The Cornishman'. Introduced into the summer timetable in 1952, this heavy thirteen coach train left Wolverhampton (Low Level) at 9.00am; initially carrying a slip coach for Taunton but subsequently a portion for Kingswear, being detached at Exeter. It travelled via Stratford-upon-Avon, Cheltenham (Malvern Road) to Bristol and was due at Penzance at 5.50pm. The northbound train left Penzance at 10.10am. It was due Plymouth North Road at 12.50pm. The arriving locomotive came off and a Laira engine came on, due to leave at 1.00pm. The train then ran non-stop to Exeter St. David's where it was due at 2.15pm. Later in the decade the departure time from Penzance was put back to 10.30am and the Kingswear portion was attached at Exeter. 'Tenby Castle' was based at Stafford Road (84A) throughout the decade. The coaching stock appears to be all ex-GWR the first coach being a Frederick Hawksworth design with domed roof-ends first introduced in 1944. *GH0618*

Image 147: Looking back towards Huntingford we are now at Michaelwood, deep in the heart of pastoral Gloucestershire as an unidentified 'Castle' coasts through with 'TRN 676'. For the summer timetables of 1956, 1957 and 1958 this number was allocated to the 2.11pm Exeter to Wolverhampton shown in the timetable as a 'Q' train (runs when required). In effect it ran in front of the 'Up' 'Cornishman' which was due to arrive at Exeter some five minutes after this train left. When the latter was heavily loaded leaving Cornwall arrangements would be put in hand to prepare this train, to ease overcrowding going forward from Exeter; hence the miscellany of coaches which makes up the train's consist. The very attractive photographic surroundings called George back a number of times; indeed on this occasion he has taken his wife Shirley with him and included her in order to lead the eye into the picture. This location is no more than a few hundred yards north of that from which he took the previous picture 146; look at the tree on the lower section of the high embankment in the background of this picture and note the comparison which links both. It is clearly late summer with a tractor at work in the field to the left of the engine. Atop the hillside is Michaelwood Lodge Farm and note too what appears to be two huts, one in each field on the hillside. *GH0347*

Image 148: We are still in exactly the same position as the previous Image 147 but now George has arranged his composition rather differently with the train going out of the picture rather than entering into it. There is much to suggest that the two photographs were taken on the same day. Close inspection suggests Shirley is wearing the same dress in both photographs and look at the tractor in the far field; is it more or less in the same place in both photographs or further progressed in this? As in the previous image the express forging south in this shot, headed by a Stanier 'Black Five', is also made up of a cross-section of ex-LMS coaches dating to each of the three Periods of the development of LMS coaching stock. Period 1 commenced after the Grouping of 1923 and lasted until the end of that decade. Counting back from the locomotive these coaches would seem to include vehicles three, seven and nine; the last nearest to the camera. The fourth carriage appears to be of Period 2 from 1930, an open vestibule with a lower waist than that of the coach in front of it. The remainder, Period 3 carriages with their familiar sliding ventilator windows and flush sides, can be attributed to the design of William Stanier from 1933 onwards. They continued to be built for several years after 1947 until the introduction of the BR Mark 1's. Note vehicles one and six have lighter roofs, a sign of newness, suggesting they were probably built in the early BR years. Could Shirley be wearing the same dress as in Image 71? *GH1360*

Image 149: The same scene again; but now time has moved on. Once more it is harvest time and the sheaves of grain in the field in the background have been gathered into stooks. The shed in the nearer field has become derelict and the goods train is headed by a much more modern locomotive than in the previous Image 148. Looking somewhat unkempt BR 'Standard Class 9' 92155 displaying a 'Class D', or if the photograph was taken post-1962, a 'Class 5' headlamp code. Either indicated a partly fitted express freight train. '92155' was a late entrant into service, delivered from Crewe Works to Saltley (21A) on 30th November 1957. By this stage of steam traction she appears not to have been very well maintained. The engine was noted in January 1961 in the Erecting Shop at Crewe Works undergoing overhaul and it may be that this picture was taken in the late summer of 1960 prior to that visit. The heavy train consists of about fifty vehicles, mainly vans. The picture was taken in bright sunshine and the shadow being cast from the west indicates it is likely to be late afternoon. The WTT for summer 1960 shows the train it is most likely to be is the 4.48pm Bristol (St. Philip's) to Leeds (Hunslet Lane) which was due through Charfield at 5.41pm and Berkeley Road South Junction at 5.47pm; although in the table that train is classified as a 'Class 4' freight. *GH1307*

Image 150: Here we have another early decade example of a Heiron panned shot. Skipping through the Michaelwood area light engine, on this occasion, is a Frederick Hawksworth 'Modified Hall' 6987 'Shervington Hall'. The fireman appears very relaxed as the engine coasts along. Looking very sprightly this youthful locomotive has probably only been in service for five or six years at the time of this photograph. She wasn't released from Swindon until 10th March 1948, three months after nationalisation, so would have been carrying the early 'British Railways' emblem on its tender from her release, rather than the **GWR** Roundel or 'Shirtbutton' monogram of earlier members of its class. From new she was sent to Gloucester (Horton Road). The **GWR** shed coding (**GLO**) was still in use at that time and it is faintly discernible on the front buffer beam between the headlamp and the nearside buffer. '6987' remained at Horton Road for four years until she was re-allocated to Worcester (85A) at the beginning of May 1952, making this picture a very early decade shot. This Class of seventy one engines was a Hawksworth development of Charles Collett's original 'Hall' Class. A number were equipped with a flat, high-sided Hawksworth tender as seen in this picture. It is said that the 'Modified Hall' Class ran freely, steamed well and were popular with both footplate and maintenance staff which may well account for the laid-back stance of the fireman in this picture! *GH0124*

Image 151: In this picture George has chosen the same rustic surroundings but has created a panorama. We are now at Lower Wick looking east to Upper Wick with the foothills of the northern Cotswolds in the background. The rising lane carries the road from Michaelwood to Upper Wick. Cutting through this panorama is a 'Black 5' 44744 heading south with a New Street to Temple Meads express. Once again, as at Wickwar (Image 145), the train is miniaturised in its surroundings. After benefitting from the favourable gradients since Berkeley Road, the engine appears to be about to open up ready for the climb to Yate. Under the 'Transport Act' of 1947, the railways became nationalised with effect from 1st January 1948. '44744' was one of those ex-LMS 'Stanier' designed locomotives, still to be released into service from Crewe Works in fledgling BR days; in this case seven months after the appointed day; on 4th July 1948. Initially allocated to Barrow Road (22A) it spent a decade bouncing between allocations there and at Leeds (Holbeck (20A) before being banished north to Liverpool (Bank Hall) (27A) in June 1958; so was one of the stalwarts on this route. Again, George has persuaded Shirley to become involved in the photograph but this time she appears at the bottom of the picture, almost hidden in the hedgerow; has she decided to go blackberry picking? *GH0136*

**Below Image 152:** A little further north we arrive at Wick Bridge which carries the lane from Michaelwood to Upper Wick across the railway. It is here that George recorded 'Jubilee' Class' 45651 'Shovell' on the 'Up' line with a northbound express. She is in extremely good order and the train she is heading, comprised of ten ex-LMS coaches is an ex-Bristol or West of England to Yorkshire express. The first coach behind the tender is a Stanier designed Brake Second (BSK) with an oval toilet window. These coaches became known as 'porthole' stock; their building actually commenced a year or two after 1947. Therefore, they were not strictly LMS stock as such but were in the direct tradition of LMS coach building practice. This coach is carrying a carriage headboard which looks suspiciously like Bradford –Bristol or Sheffield-Bristol. Although the locomotive carries no headboard the train could possibly be the 'Up' 'Devonian' or a similarly destined train. All the coaches, except perhaps for the third older vintage one, are Stanier's. Taking advantage of the falling gradient at this point 'Shovell' expels little exhaust and blows excess steam from her safety valves. She was a long term resident of Bristol (Barrow Road) (22A) from the beginning of 1953 to the end of August 1961 when she was sent north to Shrewsbury. The condition of the engine and the make-up of the train all point to this picture having been taken during the first half of the decade. More information regarding 'Shovell' was contained in Image 74. *GH0103*

**Opposite Top Image 153:** We have now arrived at Standish Junction, south of Gloucester, where the ex-Great Western main line from Swindon, here coming in from the left, joins the ex-Midland main line from Bristol. Along the latter route, in the mid-day sun; a 'Stanier Class 8F' 2-8-0 48139, with steam to spare, plods north at the head of a 'Class H' unfitted freight. The location can be identified by the agricultural over bridge in the background which carried a farm track from the A419 main road from Stroud to Gloucester across to Pidgemore Farm. '48139' is carrying what looks suspiciously like a (Toton) 18A shed code plate, a freight shed to the south-west of Nottingham. Official records do not show this locomotive ever being allocated there but between August 1955 and October 1957 it was officially allocated to Westhouses (18B), another freight shed, just a few miles further north at South Normanton in Derbyshire. Whilst the evidence of the shed plate in the photograph may deceive the eye other documentary evidence records that the engine was noted on shed on three separate occasions during the period in question sporting an 18B shed plate. Whichever the case, does this suggest the picture was taken in the middle of the decade? Perhaps the variety of coal wagons which constitute the front half of the train are empties being returned to the East Midlands coalfield. *GH0642*

**Opposite Bottom Image 154:** Crossing over to the other side of the tracks; forging north and approaching the signal box is 'Jubilee Class' 4-6-0 45577 'Bengal' heading the twelve coaches of 'The Devonian'. She is looking in fine fettle and polished even down to the front buffers. It almost looks ex-Works so may have been in for a recent overhaul. Like 'Shovell' (Image 152), 'Bengal' was another long

term resident at Barrow Road (22A), allocated there from September 1952 until becoming one of the six 'Jubilees' expelled from there in August 1961. During that period 'The Devonian' would have been one of her principal duties. The Driver looks out, almost expecting to see George at the trackside. The milepost on the left is showing 106 ¼. Being on the eastern side of the lines adjacent to the Western Region tracks, it is displaying the mileage from Paddington. Loaded to twelve coaches this looks very much like the summer train but it is interesting to note it is not double headed which leads to wondering how she coped with the 1 in 75 climb of Filton Bank out of Bristol. The fourth vehicle in the rake appears somewhat older than the rest and is likely to be a Dining Car of the LMS Period 2 Vintage. *GH0650*

Top Image 155: Viewed from beneath the Stroud to Gloucester A419 main road bridge at Standish 'Castle' 5066 'Sir Felix Pole' approaches the camera at the head of an eight coach Paddington to Gloucester express. Having come down the Gloucestershire Golden Valley from Sapperton, it now passes on the left, the same Western Region milepost seen in the previous Image 154 telling us exactly where we are. It passes a 'Down' coal train on the Midland Region main line heading towards Bristol. The train's ultimate destination would probably have been Cheltenham Spa but this engine would have been relieved at Gloucester Central by another, coming onto the train at the other end to take it forward to Cheltenham. This being one of the GWR and subsequently Western Region's principal routes, no less than five of the weekday 'Down' expresses conveyed a Restaurant Car and one a Miniature Buffet right up to and beyond the turn of the 1950/60 decade. '5066' was Old Oak Common (81A) based from its outset to demise. It was out-shopped from Swindon on the 6th August 1937 and withdrawn on 30th September 1962 after completing almost 1.3 million miles main line service. The locomotive was originally named 'Wardour Castle' but on his death, in April 1956, was renamed in memory of the late Sir Felix Pole. Pole was the General Manger of the GWR from 1921 to 1929 and as a result of his work was knighted in 1924. He is buried in the small village of Little Bedwyn in West Berkshire, where he was born on 1st February 1877. *GH0042*

Opposite Bottom Image 156: We are now on the southern side of the same road bridge looking north and have a signalman's view of a Cheltenham-Paddington express rattling over the junction at Standish. As in the previous Image 155 the engine is, once again, 5066 'Sir Felix Pole', now passing in the opposite direction and getting up a head of steam as it strikes for Stroud and the climb to Sapperton. In both photographs it has a polished boiler but the smoke box lacks a shine. The hazy atmosphere is also similar in each photograph so it is tempting to assume that both pictures may have been taken on the same day. Having arrived at Gloucester, with the first train, the locomotive would then have gone to Horton Road for servicing before heading this train back to Paddington. She is matched to a Charles Collett 4,000 gallon tender and '5066' was so equipped with three such tenders from 7th February 1950 to 21st August 1957 which fits the period of this photograph. The train comprises a rake of eight ex-Great Western coaches; the first three of which are Frederick Hawksworth designed dome-ended roof stock dating to 1944. But the most interesting is the fifth coach back, with its recessed door. This bears the hallmarks of one of the 'Super Saloons'. Designed by Charles Collett, the first eight entered service in 1931 on the 'Ocean Liner' service between Paddington and Plymouth. Subsequently twenty more 'Super-Saloon' 'Centenary' stock were built for the 'Cornish Riviera Express' of the 1930's. During the period of this photograph many of them had been subsumed into normal operational use such as the train in this picture. *GH1289*

Below Image 157: Again pictured from the signal box situated on the west side of the tracks to the south of the bridge in the previous Image 156 George captured this fine action shot of an ex-Midland 'Class 4F' 44045 charging south with a 'Class H' unfitted freight. '44045' was a long term based Gloucester engine. Delivered from Derby Works in March 1925 its early history is not known but by October 1948 it was already at Barnwood (22B) and remained operating from there until 1964. Due to boundary changes from 1st February 1958, Barnwood became (85E). After further consolidation of steam sheds on the 10th September 1960, the code was changed again, this time to (85C). Finally with the closure of Barnwood on 4th May 1964, '44045' was reallocated to Horton Road (by then 85B). One of the last highlights of its career happened on 22nd August 1963, when it was reported to have had the august duty of hauling 'Princess Coronation' 46201 'Princess Elizabeth', dead and minus some of its motion, from Saltley to the Dowty Railway Preservation Society's premises at Ashchurch; at that time a fledgling preservation centre. Shortly after moving to Horton Road '44045' clearly became surplus to requirements and was now nearly forty years old, a long service life for a steam engine. It was finally withdrawn in November 1964 and subsequently scrapped at Cashmore's, Newport the following year. '46201', of course, went on to greater things and now fully restored is in safe preservation hands. Notice the three young train spotters in short-trousers scrambling up the wooden set of steps against the bridge abutment. Has the signalman shouted a warning to them? *GH1303*

Image 158: We are now on the over-bridge featured in the previous images. From here George recorded this evocative shot of a very grimy ex-Great Western '2800 Class' 2-8-0 8F 3814 transferring from the 'Up' LM Region line to the 'Down' Western Region line in front of the diminutive ex-Midland Railway Standish Junction signal box. It is in charge of a heavy coal train loaded with up to three dozen coal wagons of various types; a typical coal train of the mid-1950's. From this type of train these engines earned their sobriquet 'Heavy Freights'. This is an early morning view, so from his north Bristol home, George was up early to set out on his travels to this point. It is a crisp morning, generating much white steam but a classic for photography. '3814' is heading a 'Class H' freight which, as may be expected with a long train of coal, is an unfitted through freight. When George Jackson Churchward became Chief Mechanical Engineer at Swindon Works in 1902 one of his first tasks was to draw up a completely new design, not based on any previous locomotive type, for hauling heavy coal trains from South Wales. The first of the '2800 Class' emerged from Swindon in 1903 and proved to be so successful that 167 were built between 1903 and 1942. '3814' was one of the later Charles Collett developments of the Class fitted with side-window cabs and other detail alterations. It was out-shopped on 11th March 1940 and had a service life of 29 years and 9 months before being withdrawn from Didcot (81E) on Boxing Day 1964. *GH1291*

Opposite Bottom Image 159: With the same cloud formation as in the previous Image 158 together with similar shadows, it appears these two shots were not only taken on the same day but close together. Here we get a good glimpse of the signal box as another ubiquitous 'Class 4F', 44558, forges north with, according to its headlamp code, a 'Class F' express freight not fitted with the continuous brake. In short this means the long rake of apparently empty coal wagons has only the locomotive brakes and the brake van in the rear to rely on, to stop the train; that would require very skilled driving and teamwork between the footplate crew and the Guard. Designed by Henry Fowler for the Midland Railway, '44558' was built by Armstrong Whitworth and delivered into the LMS stock book in April 1924 shortly after the 'Grouping' of railway companies that came into effect from the start of 1923. Records show it was allocated to Bath (Green Park) (71G) throughout the decade from nationalisation. Indeed that was where it was regularly noted by train spotters on Sunday visits right through until its withdrawal from service in December 1964 after almost forty three years service. This suggests at least part of the train originated at Bath with possibly other wagons being picked up at Westerleigh. The quadruple track work between Standish Junction and Tuffley Junction, just outside Gloucester, was unusual in that it was divided between the London Midland and Western Regions; the two lines on the east side (to the right of the picture) were Western responsibility and the two on the west were Midland. This meant the two outside tracks were both 'Up' lines', the Midland to Birmingham and the Western to Paddington whilst the two inner ones were both 'Down' lines, the Midland to Bristol and the Western to Gloucester. Whilst it sounds complicated it worked harmoniously with the signalman at Standish having control of all four. *GH1295*

Above Image 160: Approaching Standish Junction from the north on the 'Up' Western Region main line is what convincingly looks like Collett designed ex-GWR 'Grange' 4-6-0 6845 'Paviland Grange' in charge of a 'Class E' express freight with not less than four vacuum braked vehicles piped to the engine; in this case the vans immediately behind the tender. Hurrying south, she is steaming well, as her exhaust testifies. Perhaps it is late summer with a chill air creating the atmosphere for this photograph. The 'Granges' were built as mixed traffic locomotives to replace the '4300' Class. One hundred of the earlier examples of that class were withdrawn between 1936 and 1939. The wheels, valve motion and tenders were taken from the withdrawn engines, reconditioned and then used in the construction of the new 'Grange Class'. Effectively they were a smaller-wheeled version of the 'Hall Class' engines; their normal duties being freight work. 'Paviland Grange' was out-shopped from Swindon in October 1937 and during the early years of the 1950's was based at Bristol (St Philips Marsh) (82B), predominantly a freight shed, from the beginning of 1951 until October 1955. A Bristol engine in charge of the train gives a good indication where it may be heading. If that were to be the case the freight would likely be making use of the crossover (seen in images 158 & 159) onto the 'Down' Midland Region line in order to continue its journey. *GH0079*

Image 161: At the southern end of Gloucester (Eastgate) station was Barton Street Level Crossing and adjacent to it Barton Street Junction signal box sitting on a gantry above the tracks. In this classic view of the crossing an 'ex-Midland 2P Class' 4-4-0 40426 pilots an unidentified 'Black 5' out of the station with a heavy express for Bristol. The '2P' is carrying a Barrow Road (22A) shed code plate. It was allocated here from October 1951 until it was withdrawn on 26th October 1957, which makes this a photograph taken in the middle of the decade; quite possibly on the same day as the following Image 162. This engine was one of the original Samuel Johnson built locomotives entering service from Derby Works in September 1896 so having a service life of just over sixty one years. Apart from the Level Crossing, Barton Street box controlled access to the High Orchard goods line down to Gloucester Docks. But the crossing was in the middle of the city with all the consequences that carried and the road lobby wanted level crossings in the city to be removed. It was because of the cramped space available that the signal box was placed where it was, but with the increase in car ownership during the 1960's level crossings, particularly in city centres, became increasingly disruptive to life in general. The cramped space is illustrated by the close proximity to the railway of All Saints Church, on the right. It was designed by Sir George Gilbert Scott; a leading architect of his day who, in the context of railways, also designed the Midland Grand Hotel at St. Pancras station in London. Note the 'wicket gates', on either side of the tracks. On crossings immediately adjacent to signal boxes these permitted pedestrians to continue to cross the rails after the gates were closed to vehicular traffic, only becoming locked by the signalman on approach of a train. Eastgate Station and the surrounding railway infrastructure closed in December 1975. GH0005

Image 162: We now have a classic view of a busy Gloucester (Eastgate) station taken in summer 1956. The focus of course is the special train in the main 'Up' platform but perhaps of equal interest are the passengers on the 'Down' platform. There are' Scouts' in short trousers, or are they the 'Boys Brigade'? On the extreme left the outfit is much more military, so both sets are possibly off to or returning from summer camps. Beyond, in the background, a lady descends the steps from the footbridge leading to Platform 3 and the ex-GWR station, Gloucester Central. The sign actually reads 'West of England, Bournemouth and Western Station' the latter referring to the long footbridge to Gloucester Central. Surely this had to be one of the longest footbridges in Britain? In Platform 3 stands a 'Stephenson Locomotive Society' Dursley Branch special train commemorating the centenary of the Coaley to Dursley Railway which gives us the precise date, 25th August 1956. An ex-LMS Ivatt designed 'Class 2' 2-6-2T 41208 is heading the train, comprising three corridor coaches. At the time of the photograph it had just finished a five and a half year stint allocated to Barrow Road (22A) before moving across Bristol to St. Philip's Marsh (82B). The train left Eastgate at 2.50pm aided along the branch by two Johnson – Midland 'Class 1F' 0-6-0T's on what transpired to be a wet afternoon. The Cam and Dursley branch left the Bristol to Gloucester line at Coaley Junction between Stonehouse and Berkeley Road. It soldiered on for another six years after its centenary before closing to passengers on 10th September 1962. This picture emphasises the role railways continued to play during the post WWII decade; before the proliferation of general car ownership. *GH0006*

Image 163: This view of Platform 2 at Eastgate station was taken from the steps of the footbridge seen in the previous Image 162. The reason why it looks relatively deserted is because the train in the platform is already loaded and ready for departure; passengers are looking out of windows on the train in expectation. A platform ticket holder is still bidding farewell at one of the coach windows and station staff are readying themselves for departure of the train, the second from the camera is probably the Platform Inspector. Other passengers are still arriving or awaiting the next departure. Note the only remaining door open is at the rear of the train and the Guard stands well back from it because of the curving nature of the platform. The staff lining up in front of him are positioning themselves so as to signal back to the Guard that all doors are secured before he is able to 'blow the whistle' (See Image 13 for similar circumstances). Close scrutiny of the photograph discloses that the sticker in the foremost carriage window states Sheffield. The platform clock stands at 1.45pm and traditionally throughout the decade the northbound 'Devonian' was due to leave Eastgate at about this time. In the 1952 summer timetable this was 1.38pm and in the Western 1960/61 timetable it was 1.35pm. No wonder the staff are anxious to get the train away. Socially it is very much a snapshot of its period. Parcels and trunks swamp the barrows in the background, Passengers hover around the ticket collectors booth at the exit and a mother transports her young child in a pushchair of the times. See Image 98 for a Heiron comparison. *GH0008*

Image 164: Probably taken during the middle of the decade we now have a really expansive view of the north end of Gloucester (Eastgate) station. This photograph would have been taken from the very long footbridge connecting Gloucester (Eastgate) and Central stations. The focal point is a northbound express comprising a mixture of ex-LMS coaching stock, leaving Platform 2 at Eastgate behind an unidentified locomotive. Coming into the picture from the left are the Western lines from Central station controlled by Gloucester East signal box. Then comes the ex-Great Western shed, Horton Road (85B); lasting to the end of steam on the Western Region closing on 1st January 1966. To the right of the departing train is the LMR Passenger Station signal box and beyond that to the right and rather more elevated is the LMR Goods Junction signal box. One of the prominent features of the photograph is the predominance of horse box vehicles in the foreground, illustrating what a busy, strategic and agricultural area Gloucester served. In the foreground, standing in Platform 1, the 'Up' bay, is an ex-Midland 'Class 2P 4-4-0 at the head of a stopping train waiting to follow the express out of the station, probably for New Street. Close scrutiny of the photograph indicates this engine may very well be '40489', one of the Samuel Johnson designed ex-Midland Railway 'Compounds' released from Derby in May 1919. It was amongst the earliest locomotives to have the new 'lion and wheel' crest applied to its tender at Derby Works in November 1949. It was allocated to Barnwood (22B) from October 1952 until it was withdrawn in July 1960. Just look at the stack of coal on the tender. The background is dominated by the ghostly outline of the Cotswolds. *GH0011*

Above Image 165: On the south-western edge of Cheltenham lies Up Hatherley, where a footbridge known locally as 'Cloddymore Footbridge', spans the tracks. Viewed from the north-eastern side of the line we see 'Jubilee' 45651 'Shovell' passing beneath the bridge. We have seen this Barrow Road (22A) based engine before in Images 74 and 152. Here it is heading a northbound express, the first two vehicles of which are ex-LNER Gresley designed dome ended teak coaches. These probably betray the destination of the train as the Eastern Region; 'Shovell' would likely be working this train as far as Derby. The section of line between Engine Shed Junction at Gloucester and Lansdown Junction, Cheltenham was quadrupled in 1942 to cope with the increase in traffic generated by WWII. With both LMS and GWR trains using the section the necessities of the time did not give any consideration as to respective ownership by each company; though it remained jointly used until nationalisation in 1948. The introduction provided for new 'Up' and 'Down' relief lines. In this photograph the configuration of each of the four is, from the nearside, 'Up' Relief, 'Up' Fast, 'Down' Fast, 'Down' Relief. Therefore there is an anomaly to the picture; the train is running on a track, the signal for which appears to be facing the wrong way. Perhaps the answer is that 'single-line working' was in operation due to engineering works. In such circumstances specific instructions applied, involving a 'Pilotman' for safety reasons. The driver was not allowed to enter the single line section until he was in possession of a 'single line working ticket' and had authority to move from the 'Pilotman' who travelled with him through the section until the train regained its normal route. *GH1168*

Opposite Top Image 166: George has now climbed up the steps to the footbridge seen in the previous Image 165 and from the same side of the lines took this view looking towards Hatherley Junction Signal Box. This box controlled access/egress to the Hatherley Loop connecting the GWR Banbury and Cheltenham and M & SWJR routes, with the southbound Cheltenham to Gloucester main line. He has captured a very smart looking 'Black Five' 44941 displaying TRN 'W860', a train which cannot be identified by the writer. With its 'W' prefix it may be expected that this train should be running south but as with the previous image it is actually running north. Again single-line working is in operation, suggesting both pictures were taken on the same day. Close inspection of the photograph reveals the locomotive to be displaying what looks suspiciously like a (9A) shed code plate. '44941' was based at Manchester (Longsight) (9A) from October 1952 until it was re-allocated to Derby (17A) in June 1958. The 'TRN' displayed must be an LMR number, since no connecting' TRN' can be found in Western Region records. The other intriguing facet of the picture is the fourth vehicle behind the tender; which appears to be a Restaurant/Kitchen Car. If this train was an ordinary summer extra of the period it would rarely include such a vehicle. But this could just as well be an unusual appearance of the locomotive on this route. Equally it may also give a clue as to where the train is bound. It appears the Hatherley Loop was little used in later years and Hatherley Junction signal box was taken out of use on the weekend of 19th/20th November 1966 with the introduction of Stage 1A (Lansdown Junction to Churchdown) of the Gloucester Multi-Aspect Signalling scheme. *GH0652*

Right Image 167: Taken from the Gloucester Road Bridge at the northern end of Cheltenham Spa (Lansdown Road) station George captures an unidentified 'BR Standard Class 5' making a spirited, if somewhat smoky, departure with the 'Up' 'Devonian'. The locomotive does not look too healthy but, according to Peter Smith, in his book 'Mendips Engineman'(published by OPC 1972) the 'Standard Black Fives', which he fired over the Somerset and Dorset during the 1950's and early 1960's, were the 'Rolls-Royce' of locomotives (See Image 58). This particular engine hardly looks like it now. The two leading coaches are both of ex-LMSR design in full maroon livery. Beyond the engine's exhaust, at the head of one of the rake of coaches in Alstone sidings, an ex-Southern Railway 2-6-0 locomotive can just be glimpsed. Surely this would be the stock for an upcoming working over the ex-Midland and South-Western Junction line to Andover and Southampton. That being the case this photograph must have been taken prior to 11th September 1961 when that line was closed to passenger traffic. Given that information and the fact that during this period the 'Up' 'Devonian' was due at Cheltenham around 2.00pm; that information would enable experts to determine which train this could be forming. As an adjunct; some years ago in the 'Derby Telegraph' newspaper, a retired railwayman Ron Prince, 78, looked back on his years driving locomotives pulling the 'Cornishman' and 'Devonian' expresses in the 1960s. Here is what he had to relate: "The Derby crew who had worked the westbound 'Devonian', after taking their London Midland Region loco onto the MPD (i.e. Barrow Road) took a fresh loco to work the northbound 'Devonian' from Bristol Temple Meads to Bradford via Birmingham and Derby, getting relieved at Derby by Eastern Region crews". A long day out, or was this in fact a double home working? *GH1171*

Image 168: The driver of 'Black Five' 44806 has brought his engine to a stand in Bromsgrove station in readiness for the banker to be attached in the rear before setting out for the Lickey Incline. A footplate man looks back to see how things are proceeding. It appears the two banking engines are two of the ex-GWR '94xx' Class' and a number of interested faces are looking out from windows along the twelve coach train of BR Mark 1 coaches to see what the holdup is. The picture illustrates what an important hub Bromsgrove was in the days of steam. To the right of the signal gantry in the background is the three road brick shed which accommodated the banking engines stationed here. '44806' has 'TRN 1M18' chalked onto its smoke box door. For the introduction of the summer timetable in 1960 Train Reporting Numbers were fully revised to become inter-regional. 'M18' had been introduced as the designation for the 8.40am (SO) Paignton to Nottingham. In the previous year the same train was carrying Western Region 'TRN 824'. From the summer timetable 1960 the modern full four digit 'TRN's' began to be set up nationally but they only came into use gradually until full coding was introduced from 18th June 1962. '44806' was allocated to Nottingham (16A) between November 1957 and September 1964 indicating the engine would probably have worked the train from Temple Meads all the way through to Nottingham. So this photograph would likely to have been taken during the summer of 1963 or 1964. *GH1209*

Image 169: **O**ne of the locations which was almost at the limit of **G**eorge's northerly exploits was the **L**ickey **I**ncline in **W**orcestershire. **C**onstructed originally for the **B**irmingham and **G**loucester **R**ailway in 1840 this is the steepest sustained main-line incline in **B**ritain. **B**ecause of the need for heavy trains, both passenger and freight, to require assistance in climbing the bank, in 1919 **J**ames **A**nderson, acting **CME** whilst **H**enry **F**owler was concentrating on **WW1** work, designed a single '0-10-0' locomotive for the **M**idland **R**ailway specifically for banking duties on the **L**ickey. **O**riginally numbered '22290' in its **LMS** days it became '58100' after nationalisation. **S**ometime during the first half of the 1950's **G**eorge captured the engine working furiously to assist a northbound express up the bank. '**B**ertha' was the only locomotive of its kind in the world. **I**ts cylinders were of special interest because of their unique design, which incorporated cross ports and made it possible for one piston valve to supply steam to both cylinders. **A**ccording to the recollections of one retired **B**romsgrove driver '**B**ig **B**ertha' was equal to two of the '**J**inty's' (small tank engines). **T**he practice was, for the **D**river/**F**ireman of a northbound train passing **S**toke **W**orks **B**ox (approx 2 miles south of **B**romsgrove), to 'whistle' the number of locomotives he required to assist, dependent upon the state of his steam; one whistle per '**J**inty'. **S**toke **W**orks then conveyed that to the **S**outh **Y**ard at **B**romsgrove and the appropriate number was ushered up for the duty. **A**fter thirty seven years of such duties '**B**ertha' was withdrawn in **M**ay 1956 and scrapped at **D**erby **W**orks in **S**eptember 1957, having covered 838,856 miles mostly on the **L**ickey. *GH1240*

Image 170: Not all banking duties could be covered by a single engine and from the early 1930s' and quite probably sooner a small fleet of Henry Fowler designed 'Class 3F' 0-6-0 Tank Engines (Jinty's) were stabled at Bromsgrove (21C) to assist with this traffic. Here George has caught two of them getting into their stride assisting a passenger train up the bank. The two are looking very sprightly with polished smoke boxes and chimneys. During the first half of the decade the Bromsgrove fleet numbered around half a dozen. The leading engine is '47425' and the other '47303'. The Class, originally introduced in 1924, represented the ultimate development of the Midland Railway's six-coupled tank engines. It is claimed they could reach a speed of up to 60mph! '47425' was built at Vulcan Foundry and released into service in December 1926. '47303' was slightly older being delivered from Hunslet Engineering Company in January 1925. Note the apparent slight variation in the design of the cabs. Both engines had been allocated to Bromsgrove from before Nationalisation. By the middle of the decade the 'Jinty's' were getting on for 30 years service and change was in the air; Regional boundary changes were coming over the horizon. On 29th June 1956 an ex-GWR Pannier Tank '8402' piloted the 2.10pm ex-Bristol between Bromsgrove and New Street and in August became permanently allocated to Bromsgrove. The 'Jinty's' were becoming surplus to requirements. Both of these engines were re-allocated to Newton Heath (26A) in December of the same year. *GH1238*

Opposite Bottom Image 171: The 'Jinty's' were gradually replaced by more ex-GWR '94xx Class' locomotives; by April 1957 there were four and after the introduction of boundary changes in 1958, when Bromsgrove became (85F), they became eight. Not unsurprisingly, with its natural geography requiring steam locomotives of northbound trains to work flat out, the Lickey delivered outstanding action shots. During the second half of the decade George was still drawn back. He was now in an entirely different location; one that produced very artistic results. This is what you might call a beautifully framed and perfectly timed picture. A photographer may wait years for this chance to happen. Here we see what is arguably one of the first main line express passenger diesel locomotives to be introduced. A BR 1Co-Co1 Type 4 'Peak Class' diesel rolls down the incline with a Birmingham to Bristol express and passes an 'Up' express bound for New Street being assisted by a pair of these ex-GWR Pannier Tanks. The 'Peak' carries a double digit number, 'Dxx' which makes it one of the early deliveries of such engines, first introduced in 1960. If we combine their introduction with the demise of the Pannier Tanks on this route this must be an early 1960's picture. When working in pairs the banking tank engines would control their operations by a complicated system of whistle codes known only to the enginemen; all now consigned to history. But just take a moment with the photograph; the sky is calm, the field is golden, the bushes are beginning to bear fruit, everything is at peace with the world. Where else would you rather be? George has captured it all. *GH1226*

Below Image 172: What an artistic photograph this is. The cloud effect doesn't just blend with the picture but dominates it. The exhaust of locomotives both front and back merge into the scattered cumulous clouds of a quiet and still late summer afternoon. The two bankers at the rear are working furiously to help the train engine at the front. The rake of ex-LMS coaches is anything between a ten or twelve coach formation. George uses his artistic eye to include two young ladies in the foreground to bring perspective to the picture. One, dressed in a two piece suit of the day, is perched on the top of a fence rail; the other in a light coat stands alongside. Their attire perhaps indicates there is coolness in the air. Both give added interest to the scene as they watch the train go by; the driver looks out appreciatively. I suspect the lady standing is George's wife, Shirley, who has brought along a friend for a day out with George. It is just as well the sun is shining! The locomotive, a 'Black Five' 45407 carries a 'TRN 256' in printed label form, above the front buffer beam. This is a London Midland Region code, probably added at Bristol. Not looking in its best condition '45407' was allocated to Saltley (21A) between November 1954 and March 1956; which, in this mid-decade picture, probably indicates it is working its way home to Birmingham. *GH0468*

Image 173: The Lickey Incline had a continuous gradient of 1 in 37.5 for just over two miles, at the top of which was the small station of Blackwell and just beyond came the summit of the Gloucester to Birmingham line at an altitude of 564 feet. The position from which this picture is taken gives a great impression of the severity of the grade as the curvature of the track demonstrates. A look at the railway infrastructure seen in the photograph signifies the importance of this location. On the right is a quite substantial railway cottage whilst to the left are swan neck gaslights for night-time illumination and associated maintenance buildings. The 'Down' home signals must be the Blackwell starter and its repeater beyond. Alongside the repeater is the permanent speed restriction sign of 40 mph for trains descending the bank. Another 'Black Five' 44660 is still working flat out to drag its train, 'TRN 1M19' over the summit before easing the regulator. Alas the writer has been unable to determine which train this code referred to, but it does follow on directly to that of 'TRN 1M18' in Image 170 and within the sequence of George's photographs, was probably taken on the same day. Because '44660' was one of the ubiquitous eight hundred and forty two 'Black Fives' produced, there appears to be no official record of its working history. However, anecdotal evidence shows that throughout its career from 1950 to 1964 it was consistently noted at various locations always displaying a Saltley (21A) shed code plate. Even into 1964, when it was noted at Bristol (Barrow Road)(by then 82E), it displayed a '2E' shed plate which by then, due to regional changes, was the code for Saltley. So we can only assume its destination was probably somewhere in the West Midlands but as to where is a matter of conjecture. '44660' was withdrawn in September 1964. *GH1211*

Image 174: The signalman greets a footplate man as a stopping train runs into Blackwell behind a clean 'Black Five', 44966. The engine, displaying a Saltley (21A) shed code plate, was well versed with this route. Entering service from Horwich Works in August 1946; it went straight to Saltley and remained there until April 1964, apart from one short spell of five months at Bristol (Barrow Road) in the middle of the decade. At least one passenger looks out from the train as if he intends to alight. The 'Up' platform, which begins just out of picture to the left, was staggered and much shorter than the 'Down' that the train is entering. But the station entrance was through the main station building on the 'Up' side. There being no footbridge, passengers had to use a foot crossing at the south end of the station. Because the foot crossing would probably be fouled by the engine those passengers would not be able to cross the line until the train has departed. Beyond the Signal Box was the 'Up' loop into which the banking engines could run before returning to Bromsgrove. In the 1963 summer passenger timetable Blackwell was served each weekday by six 'Up' and eight 'Down' trains on the stopping service between Birmingham (New Street) and Worcester (Shrub Hill). From the shadow cast by the platform canopy it appears this train could be the 2.11pm from New Street due Blackwell at 2.39pm. The station closed in 1966. *GH1203*

Image 175: When 'Big Bertha' was withdrawn on the 19th May 1956 it was replaced by a new BR 'Standard Class 9F' 2-10-0 92079 which had only been delivered into service at Toton (18A), from Crewe Works, on 29th March 1956 and after 'running-in' was transferred to Bromsgrove (21C) a few weeks later. The electric headlight and equipment which had been fitted after 'Bertha' had been put into service was then purported to have been transferred to '92079', which had taken over the duties formerly carried out by No. 58100. The cabside number of the engine in this picture looks suspiciously like '92079' but the headlamp is either obscured by the coach or has, by this period, been removed. The passenger looking out of the corridor window has a very disdainful look on his face as he spots George crouching at the lineside. The footplateman, leaning out of his cab, also displays an equally concerned look. This locomotive remained on these duties until autumn 1963 when it was transferred away to Birkenhead (Mollington Street) (then 8H). Banking engines on the Lickey largely fell out of use with the introduction of advanced braking systems and diesel and electric locomotives. In the summer of 1988 when the Bristol to Scotland sleeper was modified to have two portions from Poole and Plymouth, which joined at Birmingham, regular banking of passenger trains ceased. Banking of freight trains on the Lickey Incline continued using a pool of specialised 'Class 66' diesel-electric locomotives. '92079' was withdrawn from service at Speke Junction shed, Liverpool (8C), where it was then allocated, on 11th November 1967 during the evening of steam when such engines were finally eliminated from British Railways in August 1968. *GH1213*